MESSAGES
FROM THE EMBERS

From Devastation to Hope:
Australian Bushfire Poetry Anthology

Edited by
Julia Kaylock and Denise O'Hagan

© Black Quill Press 2020

First published 2020
by Black Quill Press, Sydney
info@blackquillpress.com

All rights reserved. Copyright of individual poems remains with the poets. No part of this book may be reproduced or transmitted in any form or by any means, electronic, mechanical, including photocopying, recording or by any information storage and retrieval system, without the prior written permission of the publisher.

ISBN 978-0-6480020-6-2 (print)
ISBN 978-0-6480020-7-9 (ebook)

 A catalogue record for this work is available from the National Library of Australia

Cover design by Karen McDermott.

Front cover artwork by Carmel Hourigan, based on a photograph by Helen Gamble of her family home at Rosedale which was destroyed in the January 2020 fires.

Back cover artwork: 'Koala after the Fires' by Julia Kaylock.

Printed and bound in Australia.

This book is dedicated to all those directly and indirectly affected by the Australian bushfires of 2019–2020, as well as those who provided support and relief.

All profits from sales of this anthology will be directed to BlazeAid, in support of the invaluable relief work they do around Australia.

Helping Communities Rebuild After Natural Disasters Since 2009
FIRE - FLOOD - DROUGHT - CYCLONE

With thanks

We would like to thank the following people who gave their time and skills so graciously to help bring this anthology to fruition:

Amanda Anastasi, for reading the book in the early stages of production and for contributing the wonderful Foreword;

Helen Gamble, for supplying the original photo, and Carmel Hourigan for her artistic rendering of *The Rosedale House* on the front cover (you can read the story of the house towards the end of the book);

Karen McDermott, for designing the book cover and for assisting us to bring the book to life;

Euan Mitchell, for providing help with all the small pre-press details that make such a big difference;

and, of course, all the poets who sent in their work; we were humbled by the incredible response we received, and felt privileged to see the disaster through such diverse lenses.

About the editors

Julia Kaylock lives in Victoria. With a background in adult education, career coaching and educational publishing, Julia has been published widely in newspapers, journals, magazines, and online. Her poems, short stories and microfiction pieces have appeared on websites and in several publications including *The Blue Nib* (Issue 41, 2020). Julia edited the anthology *Gatherings by the Lighthouse* (Picklepoetry, 2019). Her book, *Adopting Me: A Memoir in Verse* is due for publication in late 2020. www.juliakaylock.com

Denise O'Hagan was born in Rome and lives in Sydney. With a background in commercial book publishing in the UK and Australia, Denise works as an editor with independent authors, and is Poetry Editor for Australia/New Zealand for Irish literary journal *The Blue Nib*. Her poetry is published widely and has received numerous awards. She is the author of the *Mini Style Guide* (Black Quill Press, 2018) and poetry collection *The Beating Heart* (Ginninderra Press, August 2020). https://denise-ohagan.com/

Foreword

The images and stories flashing across our TV and phone screens throughout the Australian bushfire crisis in 2019–2020 are imprinted on many of our minds – the Mallacoota residents fleeing to the shoreline, the burnt-out husks of cars, the shrieking koalas. The stress, loss and grief was brutal and life-altering for those on the frontline and anxiety-inducing for those observing from smoky inner cities and suburbia. *Messages from the Embers* encompasses a range of unique perspectives and narratives from poets across the country.

Poetry brings us into the singular, internal world of a crisis in a way a photograph, interview or news piece cannot. There is the sensory element of poetic language and a certain intimacy of tone and voice. The most memorable poems combine clarity and originality of language, deep thinking and emotional presence in a way that can be incredibly moving. For those caught up or affected by the Australian bushfire crisis, the attempt to articulate the emotional, spiritual and social toll of a catastrophe so close to home and on such a vast scale can be challenging.

Within this collection, there are sights and sounds that could only have been viewed or heard on the ground, such as the blue 'asbestos sealant on odd walls', the 'dinging Vic Emergency phone' app, the garden gnomes that survived and the burning of everyday household objects and trinkets – the disintegrated remnants of the old life. The personal connection people feel to elements of the natural world is well-depicted, such as losing a tree associated with childhood. Particularly poignant are the images of children and babies caught up in environmental destruction.

Some of Australia's best, award-winning poets are compiled in this collection, alongside new and emerging poets, all applying their unique ability to direct our focus to one or several elements of the dreadful scene confronting them. In the midst of chaos, the poet provides the quiet eye in the storm and the subsequent reflection needed. While some of the poets react to subtle, preliminary changes in the environment, others span the sweeping devastation. The dryness of both air and landscape is palpably conveyed and various portrayals of the 'new normal' and this face-masked age. There is an inherent understanding that a new landscape and reality has arrived in which we must now conduct our everyday lives.

In the 'Prelude' section, we are presented with remembrances of normality and moments that celebrate nature's beauty, followed by a turning and disturbance to the idyll. The threat of engulfing flames, harsh heat at the doorstep, burning plants, singed fur and the ash poisoning of fish follow, among other images. The poets speak of changed streets, a disrupted summer, the difficult air. Nature is often personified, and the human body becomes a metaphor for various elements of nature on fire. Occasionally, a dark humour arises – the absurdity of a smoke alarm going off in a shop or the wish to light up a cigarette.

There is a feeling in so many of the poems of persistence in hardship, including odes to firefighters. There are feelings of guilt expressed for surviving when others have not, and the mixed emotions involved in abandoning one's home and neighbourhood. Indigenous connection with the land is often touched upon and there is a palpable 'aching for country' in many of the pieces. References to the 'apocalypse' are prevalent, as are references to contemporary dystopian depictions. Throughout the collection, there is the distinct message of the weather never having been as extreme; of something utterly and irretrievably out of balance. People find themselves compelled to return to a more basic, drastically changed way of life. The politics of the time is made frequent reference to, particularly in relation to the late response of our leader and the perceived negligence, denial and spin.

In the latter section of the book, the pressing question is: What does the future hold? These poems – ranging from Cobargo to Glenbrook to Mallacoota to the living rooms of city dwellers – are just a part of the broader climate change experience for Australians and communities worldwide. The power of personal stories at a localised, domestic level of extreme weather events cannot be underestimated. These relatable, intimate 'messages from the embers' have the capacity to elicit a kind of emotion and compassion more likely to stir a climate sceptic's empathy than an online debate or partisan political oration.

Messages from the Embers concludes with a section entitled 'Hope'. We are presented with scenes of new foliage sprouting from black trunks, the exhaustion after the firefight and the resulting exhales of grief. There is the sewing of pouches for surviving joeys and the applying of salve to burnt paws – the marks that the fires have left on skin, fur, feathers, plant life and land, the cooling ash, the endurance, the loss, and the images of trauma and gradual healing. There are birds singing after the smoke has cleared and nature finding its way back, along with a desire for a changed, more perceptive way forward.

Amanda Anastasi
Poet in Residence,
Monash Climate Change Communication Research Hub

Contents

Foreword	ix
Backdrop	xxi
Introduction	xxiii

PART ONE: PRELUDE	1
Forest tracks, *Robyn Sykes*	3
Dry, *Emma Briggs*	4
Drought sonnet, 26.11.19, *Helen Moore*	5
Crowdy Head before fire, *Margaret Bradstock*	6
Pre-Pyrocene, *Simone King*	8
Aching for country, *George Clark*	9
Frightening extremes, *Tony DeLorger*	10
Black feathers, *Rosa O'Kane*	11
Nunyara, *Dave Kavanagh*	12
Northern Victoria, *John Lowe*	13
Drought still, *Julian O'Dea*	
Climate of fear, *Tegan Jane Schetrumpf*	14
Holidaying on Kangaroo Island, *Audrey Molloy*	15
Pyromaniac's lament, *Peter Mitchell*	16
Circuit, Blackheath, *Kathryn Fry*	18
Fire in my heart, *Adèle Ogiér Jones*	19
why are we not ready for this? *Sandra Renew*	20

Bitter orange @2 am, *Linda Adair*	21
Dusk flight, *Diana Pearce*	22
This, *Ash Spring*	23
No regrets, *Ava Mendoza*	24
Regulation, *Angela Costi*	26
Dicing with fire, *Virginia Lowe*	27
Hidden, *Fotoula Reyolds*	28
Road trip, *Daragh Byrne*	29
Ash drops into the courtyard, *Rebecca Trowbridge*	30
Battle ground, *Ellen Shelley*	31
ember attack, *Kit Kelen*	32

PART TWO: DEVASTATION — 35

State of Emergency, *Cheryl Pearson*	37
This is not a drill, *Anne Casey*	38
When Australia burned, *Steve Boyce*	40
The thought, *Jeltje Fanoy*	41
Her bush un-settlement, *Susan Wakefield*	42
Fire, *Gaylene Carbis*	44
Goodbye cruel world, *Lance Convey*	44
Unless water kills, *Rob Schackne*	45
Silvam incendit, *Juleigh Howard-Hobson*	46
Currowan fire, *Dorothy Swoope*	47
Dawn of fire, *Kathleen Panettieri*	48
Waiting to rescue, *Jane Baker*	50
Orange moons, *Robin Purdey*	51

Hi-Viz heroes, *Sam Middleton*	52
Volunteer firefighter, *Julie Annette King*	54
As mates, *Jai Thoolen*	55
Facing the beast, *Vacen Taylor*	56
Fire this time, *Linda K. Menzies*	57
Blue Mountains (Leura), *Mark Roberts*	58
48°C, *Brenda Proudfoot*	60
Sentinel, *Darrell Coggins*	61
Climate revolt, *Carolyn Gerrish*	62
Bushfire haiku, *Robin Purdey*	64
I love a sunburnt country, *Niel Smith*	66
Work clothes, *Patricia O'Gready*	68
Gnangara fires, *Siobhan Hodge*	70
It didn't start this way, *Mary Chydiriotis*	72
Air purifier, *KL Morris*	73
Evacuation, *Kirily Isherwood*	74
Devastation 2020, *Lilian Cohen*	76
Tanka, *Michelle Brock*	77
ice fire stone, *Nick Allen*	77
How to protect the lungs, *Ivy Ireland*	78
Koala in flight from bushfire, *Barbara Petrie*	80
rigor mortis, *Susan Hawthorne*	81
Thirteen ways of sighing in an ecocide, *Toby Davidson*	82
Fire through the screens, *Siobhan Hodge*	84
White peaches, *Moya Pacey*	85
Leaving Canberra, *Hazel Hall*	86

A new normal, *Mark Roberts*	87
Sunshine Coast to Sydney, *Rosie Jackson*	88
Wildfire, *Gary Colombo De Piazzi*	89
Bushfire moon, *Ron C. Moss*	90

PART THREE: AFTERMATH	93
Refugee, *Beatriz Copello*	95
Post inferno, *Tony Steven Williams*	96
No word, *David L. Flaxman*	97
City in smoke, *Erin Frances*	98
sepia sky, *Irina Frolova*	99
In the valley of dying stars, *Órlaith Ní Brádaigh*	100
Rescuing refugees, *Virginia Lowe*	101
Aboard the Choules, *Alexandra Wallis*	102
Australia visits Minnesota, *Angela Costi*	103
Lithgow, *Richard Soloway*	104
Seven snapshots of the east coast fires, *Amanda Stewart*	106
Time of dying, *Marilyn Humbert*	108
Firelife, *Gail Willems*	109
Functionality extinct, *Kelly Van Nelson*	110
Ash mounds, *Geoffrey Bonwick*	112
What's saved, *Les Wicks*	114
Chimneys, *Helen Budge*	115
How loss happens, *Geoff Callard*	116
Blue stain and silence, *Jane Baker*	117
Burning, *Chris Considine*	118

Burnt, *Dorothy Simmons*	119
The old burnt gum, *Nardine Sanderson*	120
Smoke, *Brenda Saunders*	121
Sturdy bodies, *Jane Downing*	122
Ash, *Natalie D-Napoleon*	123
Possum requiem: Ode to Mallacoota, *Milena Cifali*	124
The wind breathes, *Joe Dolce*	126
Honey, *Moya Pacey*	127
Corrugated iron, *Diana Pearce*	128
Getting used to it, *Josh Cake*	129
Roadblocks, *Anders Villani*	132
The mountain, *Anthony Lawrence*	134
Wollemi National Park, *Margaret Bradstock*	136
Saving the pines, *Louise Wakeling*	138
What would my knitting Nanna do? *Kate Lumley*	140
Heat stroke, *Barbara Petrie*	141
My Daddy, my hero, *David L. Flaxman*	142
I tried to sweep the ash away, *Cate Beresford*	143
No music, *John Lowe*	144
PART FOUR: HOPE	145
Full mast, *Kelly Van Nelson*	147
The fire has gone, *Jenny Ash*	148
Holding on, *Kathryn Sadakierski*	149
The science of kindness, *Jen Webb*	150
The green is gone, *Dorothy Swoope*	151

Scorched soul, *Leanne Dyson*	152
fire season, *Terry Wheeler*	154
The bush is still singing, *Sandra Renew*	155
Rising from the ashes, *Richard Bell*	156
Thirty days after the bushfire, *Rob McKinnon*	157
13, *James Walton*	158
Dystopian palette, *Natalie Cooke*	159
Rebirth, *Mickey Martin*	160
Strength, *Lindsay Coker*	161
a thing to do alone, *Gareth Sion Jenkins*	162
Coagulated time, *David Atkinso*	164
Optimism, *Colleen Z. Burke*	166
Aria, *Laura Jan Shore*	167
The Croajingolong Phoenix, *Colin Lanphier*	168
Forest pyre, *Cathy Soulsby*	170
I contemplate my fire, *Órlaith Ní Brádaigh*	172
And if they ask how it happened, *Laura Jan Shore*	174
Mandala, Delicate Nobby Beach, *Helen Moore*	175
Embers, *Adèle Ogiér Jones*	176
Rain and Song, *Miriam Hechtman*	177
New days, *Mark Mordue*	178
New hope, *Vacen Taylor*	180
Emblazoned, *Kathryn Sadakierski*	181
Acknowledgments	185
Biographies	187

The House at Rosedale	209
About BlazeAid	215
Afterword	219

Backdrop

Following a prolonged drought, in September 2019, the official start of the Australian bushfire season, parts of the country were already blazing. By early November a State of Emergency had been declared for Queensland and northern New South Wales, and by early 2020 fires were sweeping the country on an unprecedented scale.

Fires raged for weeks, with devastating losses to properties, natural habitats and wildlife. Australians rallied, offering homes and accommodation, food and supplies, financial assistance, counselling and welfare services, and practical support. Doctors and pharmacists provided free health services and medication; hotels, bars and cafes around the country donated their tip jars to the cause. Support poured in from abroad.

By mid-February 2020 millions of hectares of land had been burned, including important World Heritage areas. Heavy rains finally doused the flames, leaving communities, environmentalists and climate scientists to assess the damage and begin taking steps towards recovery and rehabilitation – an endeavour that will take many years. Resultant floods, however, necessitated fresh solutions to new problems. Around one billion animal and 50 human lives were lost in the fires. Thousands of homes and commercial buildings were destroyed. Livelihoods were impacted by burnt soil, stock losses and the downturn in tourism.

At around the same time, adding yet another layer of pain and loss, a pandemic was brewing – COVID-19, the effects of which are still being felt as this book goes to print. Our heartfelt condolences go to those affected, directly and indirectly, by the events of 2019–2020.

The Editors

Introduction

Ah, better the thud of the deadly gun, and the crash of the bursting shell,
Than the terrible silence where drought is fought out there in the western hell;
And better the rattle of rifles near, or the thunder on deck at sea,
Than the sound — most hellish of all to hear — of a fire where it should not be.

'The Bush Fire', Henry Lawson (1905, Stanza 1)

Bushfires have been the subject of many an Australian poem. From Banjo Paterson and Henry Lawson, through to the late great Les Murray, we have a rich history of literature recounting the devastation wreaked by fires.

The 2019–2020 fires once again provided poets far and wide with impetus to write, speak and sing their responses — which they did, in great numbers. It seemed natural to corral the best of this work into an anthology, and thus contribute to the bushfire relief program.

During the submission period we received around 350 poems — far more than could possibly be published in a single anthology. Our aim in selecting work for inclusion was to provide poetic variety (from free verse and prose poetry to more stylised forms), to showcase poets from a wide range of backgrounds and ages, and to give a real feeling for what it was like to live through the fires. Submissions arrived from around Australia and the world, from emerging poets and established voices. Some poems mourn the loss of wildlife and habitat; others are an eloquent plea for change; some speak of resilience in the face of catastrophe; still others focus on renewal. Reflecting this, we have structured the anthology in four distinct parts which provide a cohesive narrative describing the journey from forewarning to devastation and its aftermath, and finally to hope.

It has been a privilege to work with all the poets and to shine a light on their work, to unify it into a rich and varied poetic tapestry of the most devastating series of bushfires Australia has experienced. We feel honoured to have received such a wonderful array of work from the Australian and international poetry community, and present an anthology created with dedication and care. We sincerely hope you enjoy reading the poetry, and especially wish to thank all those who purchase *Messages from the Embers*, as in doing so you are contributing to the ongoing relief effort.

Julia Kaylock and Denise O'Hagan

Part One

PRELUDE

> 'The forest is a tinderbox.
> The farmers feel alone.
> The fear of fire is everywhere.'
> Emma Briggs

> 'Those were the last days of telling children
> it would all be OK'
> Simone King

> 'how little a cinder
> we'll make of
> this whole hurtling world'
> Kit Kelen

Forest tracks

Have you hiked on old-growth forest tracks in summer;
felt caresses cool as creek-song stroke your skin;
flinched at shying skinks, marked time with tree-frog
    drummer;
soaked in filtered light and cleansed the voice within?
Have you brushed the granite's biceps with your fingers;
deep-inhaled the breath of ferns, fed hungry leech;
sniffed the lemon myrtle spice that wafts and lingers;
stretched your arms across the girth of ancient beech?
The orange ogres storm and spit and scream;
spew smoke that chokes and char-grills ferns and frogs;
shoot flames that punch and melt and boil and steam
and sear the skinks, roast fungi-coated logs.
So, how can ash-streaked humans soothe the strain
when forest tracks themselves cry out for rain?

Robyn Sykes

Dry

The dams are draining dangerously.
The creeks are sticks and stones.
The ground is brown and brittle.
The leaves die one by one.
The grass is just a memory.
The insects have all gone.
The wallabies are hungry.
The cows are skin and bone.
The bats are falling from the trees.
The koalas are nearly done.
The forest is a tinderbox.
The farmers feel alone.
The fear of fire is everywhere.
The water is trucked in.
The clouds form and blow away again.
The drought goes on and on.

Emma Briggs

Drought sonnet, 26.11.19

On the coastal train Sydney to Wauchope, I see land
so barren, stripped of skin by untraditional farming
of Sheep, Cattle. Almost gone, rainforests logged
for pasture, billions of bacteria no longer seeding
clouds, forming rain – sweet, delicious rain.
Desiccated, ugly, this is Nature subservient
to industrial farming, the tyrant master driving
the consumer wish for monocultural meat;
beasts enslaved to a system that's barely scored
two centuries here, and is already waning.
Hardly a blade of grass for tongues to tug, teeth to crop;
and farmers on their knees, taking their own lives,
their kids depressed, and no surprise, being deprived
of vision – ways to work with the land, and thrive.

Helen Moore

Note: Helen Moore deliberately utilises initial capitals to elevate the status of animals and natural phenomena.

Crowdy Head before fire

They called them 'blackboys'
            back in unenlightened days.
Some still do. Standing spear-tall
erect, they fill the landscape,
            white flowers aquiver with bees
homing in on the nectar.
Once pollinated, they form a tough
            pointed fruit capsule, matt-black.
You can eat the inside part
            but it kills them, the harvesting.

As sunset's fireball doubles itself
in water, flannel flowers –
        petals ash-white as stars –
            hunker down on the headland
where winds beat them squat. Survivors,
they thrive in adversity. Yellow Isopogon,
            ornate and curious 'drumsticks',
flaunt rounded heads
        from dwarfed and tufty groundcover.

Across each photograph, dead banksias
                    weave an interlace
of blackened branches, hardy as wrought iron.
Burnt in the last fire, they release
                    their seeds to fall on ground
well fertilised with ash. Some
won't shed unless there is a fire.
                    Wizened banksia cones perch
like black cockatoos, stand sentinel
                    along skeletal limbs.

Margaret Bradstock

Pre-Pyrocene

Those were the last days of running
nowhere in particular, of feeling the salt
lace your brow, the endorphins flush your blood
like clean ice water. The last of breathing
without worry, without imagining
the particles' foul course through your body,
organ by exhausted organ.

Those were the last days of a sun
too bright to look at directly,
but dispersed and invisible like a God.
Now, in sky cloaked and cloudy-grey,
a sly red disc rides the murk.
You squint now to make out closer things –
your neighbours hurrying their children,
face-masked, into cars. Questioning
their parents at first, then quiet. Compliant.

Those were the last days of the mantra
'rainforest can't burn, rainforest can't burn'
even when the smoke from the north-west
signalled it was alight. The Antarctic beech,
labyrinthine roots scorched, loosened their
deep-time embrace of the earth. We too let go.

Those were the last days of telling children
it would all be OK, next summer would be better,
there would be growth, fluffy and green,
rising from the ash. The last of pretending
that life was spread out in front of them
like an endless sea-kissed summer
and like the mountains they could once see,
through clear air, at the end of their street.

Simone King

Aching for country

I am aching for my country as drought sucks love dry
Embedded here where everything seems so far away
This weather is re-wilding nature as I lie on the earth
Mixing my breath with the morning dew and give thanks
For those trees still linking the soil to the sky, while
My stubborn spirit feeds the illusion that we belong here.

The relentless logic of isobars bring the blanket of heat
Grasshoppers chewing the pasture left by herbivores,
Obeying some mysterious rule of nature, trying
To find equilibrium between geology and biology.
Farm animals born here yet not quite part of the landscape
Like the macropods who hang around until
The pasture is gone and the sale yards are full.
Finally nature destocks as well as the roos are followed
By insects and birds, leaving just the farmer and his dog.
Then with luck the northwest wind brings dust and bone
    fragments
And then moisture from the ocean of shipwreck and spice
Crossing the continent with 40,000 years of stories and songs.

The rain is coming, in its own good time, to save a few snakes,
Echidnas and dung beetles, but the creeks are underground,
And there is a smell of burnt ambition, shrouded in a cloak of
    smoke.
The heat is making nomads of us all, we are now
At the intersection of instinct and wisdom,
Where a poet wanders searching for continuity.

George Clark

Frightening extremes

Our fruit-bearing tree wilts in the temperatures,
its almost ripe fruit suddenly dried and dead
    from one harsh day,
and so many plants, even desert succulents
have been burned in nature's tirade,
their once-plump leaves woody in patches,
with deep wounds of dry twisting sinew,
and no amount of water can restore the loss,
just another cost of extreme weather.

Looking to the sky,
I wonder what next will unfold,
the face of life has changed,
even beauty is tainted, rearranged,
unable to adjust to this intensity,
like thousands of rare black cockatoos
falling dead from the trees,
heatstroke a sentence of death,
in a land where the heat of summer
has always been, but not like this.

As species fall, fire consumes
and even the air we breathe
becomes intolerable, toxic in fumes,
we are faced with the same problems
ill-addressed for so long,
and now we face losing everything,
so will humanity change,
rectify the outrageous consumption
of natural resources, our disregard
for the natural world and cycles of longevity.

Tony DeLorger

Black feathers

It's the eve of The Eve.
Redhead knocking
on the door.
The sun a pink blister.
Dirty dishwater sea
in a sandwich of sand.

Black feathers pirouette
stall before landfall –
Black leather leaves.

Rosa O'Kane

Nunyara

Listen, mother.
Cock your ear
to the voice
of your children.

Gaura is
a bristle bush
that kicks up dust,
and clouds
are spendthrift tourists.

The song of Elimatta
keens.
Patience, she pleads.

But our throats
are parched,
and gnashing jaws
crave more
than wishbones
to suckle.

Dave Kavanagh

The Indigenous word 'Nunyara' means 'restored to health' or 'breathe again'.

'Elimatta' is an Indigenous word meaning 'our home'.

Northern Victoria

A greyness fills the land,
softening hills, suffusing
every stand of bush,
turning saplings pastel,
spreading over paddocks,
all in the stillness of afternoon,
for this is no morning mist,
instead its evil twin.

A week passes:
sunlight itself, blunted blue,
mocks the name of Bright.

John Lowe

Drought still

Grey clouds promise rain
but only spit down with disdain
a few drops to sizzle on a pan
mocking us again.
Nothing to soak and sustain,
but just a trace,
a trickle on the earth
like tears on a brown face.

Julian O'Dea

Climate of fear

Near the Gospers Mountain fires

'There's a new fire in your watch zone.'
We're having a child to this
dulcet tone; as she is, due in two, she's easy
to carry and flee with.

Each time the warning pings again, I'm grateful
our beloved cat passed
in October; no need for carry-crate and tins
to be stacked by our door.

Eyes dry and stung, coughing residual phlegm
even here, where it's 'safe',
life is overcast with a pall – my thoughts turn
to the dead and unborn.

Tegan Jane Schetrumpf

Holidaying on Kangaroo Island

'the death of 20 of these marsupials would be very significant.'

We're talking about the word *devastated,*
how it has come to require qualification:
absolutely, completely, utterly,
as though a single word
were not devastating enough. We lie,
at dusk, in our rammed-earth lodge,
each end of the pared-back lounge, our legs
loosely herringboned. Two miniature
marsupials appear – dunnarts, we discover
(having ruled out the antechinus
on cuteness factor alone).
How much are they *paying?* you query.
I clap my hands and they jump three inches
mid-scamper, then flatten through the grating
of the air vents in the floor. Partial to layers
of icing in the Liquorice Allsorts in my backpack,
they leave a stack of rubbery black squares,
the merest pastel scaffold. Only thirteen pockets
of the creatures on the island, a tiny population.
    absolutely
                  completely
    utterly
That was last week, before the fires.

Audrey Molloy

* quote by Pat Hodgens, fauna ecologist, Kangaroo Island Land for Wildlife

Pyromaniac's lament

In this small town, I am a lover of fire. At six years,
matches became playthings. Strike one and revelation

arises! These flares open my long-closed eyes.
I see visions: incendiary worlds, ashes as confetti.

Bush surrounds our houses. The eucalypts were leafy
comfort & sing their secret longings: regeneration

through fire. Now I fulfil my life's coordinates.
I climb through barbed wire and walk away from

the houses. Dry grass cracks underfoot like breaking
glass. My hands join the earth: a circle of fire blooms.

I stand up and see a boy at the fence. A breeze swings
in the trees. The memory-bank ignites.

I see myself on the ground. This boy's older brothers
stand over me. *Fuckin weirdo! You should be locked up!*

The boy sees fire hands, lantern eyes. Now his legs
pound the parched earth toward the houses.

Winds pick-up, my shoulders relax. Smoke calligraphies
the gusting air. Gum trees dazzle gold; their branches

cataracts of flame. I leave my burning amours.
A nearby road is my escape. Beside me, the trees warn:

here they come! At a corner, I hear sirens.
A blue-suited grabs my shoulder; handcuffs hold

my freedom tight. *What is my crime? I am a mere
acolyte, a lover of tree destinies.* Through bars

later, I hear grass as charred remnants, blackened stumps,
birthing cries & I know my hands will light the world again.

Peter Mitchell

Circuit, Blackheath

Just yesterday there was no hint of these
tenuous doubletail orchids on stray stems

and overnight, the waratah's central bloom
morphed into steady shoots, triggered

by the promise of rain it seems. I think
how different we are, you and I, often

on separate paths. This morning, a hillside's
lit with a thousand lanterns of bauera rose

another with yellow peas in the grey light,
the air awash with peppermint oil. Whistlers

and spinebills sing up and down the track
and the creek runs louder at Boyds Beach.

We meet on this day in November, attuned to
each other at Govetts Leap, before the megafire

burns from Gospers Mountain and blazes Grose
Valley and sweeps up the cliffs at Blackheath.

Kathryn Fry

Fire in my heart

If time could stand still
it would be in peace
where the billabong
flows beside the bridge
on the border,
where the river flows
down to the gulf
where the land's smile
once coped with emotions
of lovers who gazed.

Before the rape
by greed and corporations
their fury firing
denying destruction
of wilderness peace,
infernos ignoring
all in their path
wildlife confined
in shrinking enclosures
enflamed in fires made in hell.

Adèle Ogiér Jones

why are we not ready for this?

smell the coming firestorm on the first smoky wind
pray to any available spirits for the safety of the secret
    sacred places
salvation projects in deep bushland

indigenous story webs tell of oceans rising
    destructive flooding rain
no stories sing of catastrophic fire
    no song or hymn or raging ballad
we've never seen anything like this

the smell of damp earth is sunk in disbelief
    last lost running water echoes
fire trails are frontlines in Bush Heritage country
life dried out of everything, heat spikes kill

converting hope to prayer we mourn for
    Mumbulla Mountain and Brogo bush
waterfalls and wallabies
    dry rainforest and old growth trees
    wet vine forest
    sugar gliders
    common wombats

long-nosed bandicoots
    powerful owl
    scarlet honeyeater
    native figs
    grey-headed flying fox   make record of them all
now teetering on extinction —

firestorm from Yowrie splits
    rampages down twin valleys to Quaama and Cobargo
why are we not ready for this?

Sandra Renew

Stanza 2 derived from Biamanga Board Chair Bunja Smith quoted in 'Battle for Biamanga' *Bega District News, 17 Jan. 2020.*

'Bush Heritage' refers to Brogo Reserve at the end of Bega Valley, NSW (conservation and nature reserve).

Bitter orange @ 2 am

The halfmoon slyly glowers
a chiaroscuro profile amid
cool air dulled by heavy haze
which wafts upslope from
campfires of misguided tourists
travelling to the 6th extinction
while notifications ping phones
across the sleepless valley.

Linda Adair

Dusk flight

From my balcony
I watch flying foxes
dip past,
noiseless
close,
no birds
these black velvet
curves of flight
above the city's evensong.

Elsewhere
they hang,
fold into their wings,
speak in hacksaws of sound
through dew-filled air
and slivered moonlight.

After this summer's cauldron
will they be glimpsed only in dreams
or felt in a frisson of air at dusk?

Diana Pearce

This

Green gives way to umber and charcoal
along the heat-shimmer road
A before and after photo of destruction,
playing out in real time
Life on my left and ruin on my right;
the car rolls on
Woodsmoke air fills my lungs and –
I cannot breathe
How many have been lost?
How much has been lost?
Arguments about cause and blame
go back and forth
Yes, we get bushfires, but not like this
Not like this.

Ash Spring

No regrets

The sound of fire crackling fills the air.
Distant roaring, then the fire truck crawls closer
as onlookers howl with fear and fury
The once green and alive forest
falls into a graveyard of once trees.

The 'Don't Feed the Wildlife' sign
falls to the ground
crushing what was once a cockroach home.

I try to remain silent,
but as I walk
leaves are crunching beneath my feet.

As I look up
I see an endless river of flames
indestructible waves of fire
crash over the tallest trees.

I can feel the sweat forming on my brow.
The smell of burning coal
gets more intense every minute
making it harder for fresh air to enter my lungs.

I have to move fast.
The flood of fire is moving my way.
Ashes fly onto my jeans and t-shirt
creating holes;
you can see my skin
the stench of burning flesh fills the air.

I see the distant lights of the fire truck
peeking through the thick clouds of smoke
and the roaring siren signalling
to move and that help is here.
The fire is eating away at the land,
devouring everything in its path
leaving no trace of forest behind.

I started to feel queasy
as I watched the land I grew up in crumble.
I remember what my Grandfather told me.

NO REGRETS!

But all I feel is regret and shame.
I should not have had that cigarette.

Ava Mendoza (11 years)

Regulation

The haze tends towards insomnia
giddy with release
celebrating the new year's red moon,
it will not race you to the bus
this morning, you have time to breathe
still wear your runners
walk like you're about to jog.
Don't close your gate, you may need to return
before you arrive.
There is talk of the older eucalypt
heaving with the weight of ash –
do not seek its shelter
keep away from its outstretched branches,
keep up your pace
as the haze will wake
its smoke to play
the game of seek, find, choke.
Do not take off your mask
to wipe your sweat,
keep your ears alert
do not fill with plugs to avoid
the subtle crackle and creak
of earth and air
in hot contest
for your life.

Angela Costi

Dicing with fire

'I ... am convinced He does not play dice with the universe.' Einstein.

In the city, smoke-coloured sunlight throws unexpected orange into corners of houses, flickering like flames as leaves flutter before it on the polluted air. Goddog smiles at the irony. The wide brown land beckoned fifty years ago. Sun, wind and tide for power, not a fossil fuel in sight. So did their leaders lead? Work to change the climate change? Crowned with laurel leaves as innovators? No, they built the world's biggest coal mine instead; kept accepting bribes from the giants; offering them grants from the public purse – till the sun-burnt country turned to a bush-burnt country – hectares and hectares of native forest, uplands, downlands, burnt to a crisp. Millions of iconic animals homeless, foodless, some species gone forever. Homes lost and human lives. And the leaders lead in showing how a beleaguered country lives with climate change. Doggod is here in herhis high-vis vest – exactly the same stomach-wrenching orange – disguised as a boilermaker and volunteer rural firey. As the team, hoses in hand, watch the fire front crest the hill – collecting several buildings on the way – Goddog squats by a cleared patch of road and fishes hisher dice from an inside pocket. Insectivore swarming planet Xenon awaits, but this planet is almost finished – wiped clean for a new intelligence to evolve. Will heshe wait out the result? Doggod is curious.

Virginia Lowe

Hidden

At the end of the ocean
Where the sky descends
There is nothing to see
And dreamtime is dark

The arch of my feet
Feel the air pass through
Even the softness of sand
Feels like death on earth

In the grey distance
A thick curtain obscures
An unnerving aloneness
No one dares to light up a cigarette

The colour green is dead
It burns in the back of my throat
The pleasure of the beach stings
And I swim in salt-water guilt

White surf rises and falls
Two shades of blue live
I'm relieved in the nearness
Wet skin, dry bones

Scorching sun descends
In the murky salmon-glow
And the skyline is not there
A defining no-show

Fotoula Reynolds

Road trip

I drove from Grafton down through Armidale
Deliberate, I had to see the land

The fires had visited. Not being native
Myself, I was surprised the blackened bush

Burned incompletely, leaving charred trunks and
Even some green leaves reaching from the ashes -

Something on the earth hoped to survive
At least. I worried I'd taken a wrong turn

The road through Nymboida just reopened
The dense heat of the day, the parched land

Making me restless, uncertain, tentative.
I had to drive around a damaged bridge

Grateful, then guilty, that the creek
Beneath had disappeared, the bridge unsafe

For transport, over or underside. They lost
Eighty-five houses here a month before.

Tents in the glade were not as I surmised
Holiday makers. I sped on with a sense

Of the impermanence of all of this
Clutching at the sky like a scorched tree

For a safety that's made of air, promises
We make to ourselves, imagining

If we hold on tight enough we'll beat the flames.

Daragh Byrne

Ash drops into the courtyard

Ash drops into the courtyard from a massacre,
a few towns away, held back by the firebreak
of suburbs and smokejumpers.

Upward on jets of hot wind,
each fragile mote hoped to follow
the great spirit from each flaming tree.
But Earth circles
scatters the ash in our dystopian snowglobe;
the sacred scarab rolls dung around,
nests in it.

Christmas is muted by silky grey powder
peppering priorities, for the lucky ones,
of family transactions and candy canes.
For firefighters, nurses, police
and their families at reality's front lines,
November means foreboding,
December, exhaustion. Bushfires

cast newly homeless
with drowned-island escapees
onto the tally of climate refugees
that we have all become
even by closing shutters
against unsettled orange skies.
Denial and hope comfort: germinating seeds

click pros against cons on a mental abacus
weighted towards wait-and-see, then reaction,
versus planning for consequence.

Our clacking crab-pile forms and falls:
we skitter, gab and grab
to get away but none egress
the roiling clatter-bucket.

We'd known for a while that the coast was dry.
We'd known for longer of our fragile supply.

Rebecca Trowbridge

* Eastern NSW fires, early December 2019

Battle ground

the word catastrophic has the sound of a branch cracking like guns. a sentence of violent gusts, a quickening of pulse. Air stretched like skin. the nervous system of forest & plain disembowelled from its source. debris is a fuse. a strike of defiance from above. Looting homes. the moon smoked pink. a rain gauge out of order. a false start airborne in the lungs of kookaburra. a forecast in red. stubbled troopers. Sacks full of water. clouds of smoke. we pray for less. for the grey of winter. for pelting rain. for fur that never touched a flame.

Ellen Shelley

ember attack

Crawford River Fire, December 2019, considered from Markwell, on a day declared 'catastrophic'.

how many weeks has it been, this fire?
packed and still ready to go

white sky, blue through
waiting for the wind

how many of us are there?

moon of an eerie colour
on Jarrah Rd
who's ever heard of that?

the fire won't know our names
it's as if smoking had taken us up

millions, I think
in all the outskirts, in every town
on blocks, deep in the bush

and north of us at Ghin-Doo Ee
on Cabbage Tree Mountain
(similar distance and out of control)

bats flap in the walls
wallabies eat the last lettuce

having heard of the burning spears
of the freight train un-railed

all say 'unprecedented'

we learn names of roads nobody knew

least leaf carries
a lesson of white sky, blue through

waiting for a speck, a mote
grit in the eye

how little a cinder
we'll make of
this whole hurtling world

weeks it's been for us all
still packed and ready to go

Kit Kelen

Part Two

DEVASTATION

'A continent simmers ...'
Thermometers climb into red, then redder.'
Cheryl Pearson

'It is hard to read this country now
a charcoal ash poem
that stretches into the future.'
Mark Roberts

'We are taken back to basics,
ashen-faced creepings
on the fringes of survival.'
Siobhan Hodge

State of Emergency

Bedouins saw castles where
the hot air wavered – dithering
towers, domes of bent light.

In New South Wales, the illusion
is green: foxtail palms and gums
dreamt out of a heat that sweeps

like a bridal train, black ash lacing
its wake. A row of hoses aimed
like a prayer is a thumb touched

to a colander. Too late, the Prime Minister
surrenders his lounger, leaves his pina
colada to the bees. A continent simmers.

Grief and steam. Thermometers climb
into red, then redder. Still the fires
pass on the baton: flame to flame to flame.

Cheryl Pearson

This is not a drill

Mom and daughter Robinson take off
their gas-masks as they enter the shop.
The air looks murky outside, everything
suspended in blue haze. Experts say Earth
has been hit by a meteorite (or so we think
so far). The impact was like an atomic bomb.
Vast areas engulfed in flames. Many people
have died. Or lost their homes. The military
have been deployed. Some say it is
the Apocalypse. There is no immediate
solution in sight. The nightmare continues.
This is a flashback scene. The Robinsons
are Lost in Space now. This is fiction.

The fire alarm goes off as I enter the shop.
Outside in the open-air mall a siren sounds
over and over. Over a loudspeaker a tinny
voice advises us that the fire alarm
has been activated. We are instructed
to stand by for further instructions.
After ten ear-splitting minutes,
no further instructions are issued. No-one
has stood by, much less slowed, in their hot
pursuit of bargains in the January sales.
The air quality app on my phone bleeps
a warning. It is hazardous to be outside,
breathing the suspended blue haze
that has swallowed most of Sydney.
We are not wearing gas-masks. My lungs are
burning. Experts say the wild bushfires
ravaging this country are like the impact

of an atomic bomb. Over a million hectares
engulfed in flames. Many people have died.
Or lost their homes. The military have been
deployed. My son says it is the Apocalypse.
> *Earth is trying to stop us Mum*
> *before all the animals are gone.*
There is no immediate solution in sight.
This is not a flashback scene. This is not fiction.

This is today and every other day
in Sydney since early November last year.
Watching and praying for friends
to our north, south and west fighting
to save their homes. Ordinary heroes
everywhere risking their lives. To our east,
the ocean carries smoke four hours' flight
to New Zealand. Navy ships dock
at blaze-besieged beaches to rescue
stranded families from their Christmas
escapes. We are Lost in the Space now
between when this nightmare started
and its unforeseeable end.

Anne Casey

5 January 2020, Sydney

When Australia burned

Hazy Sunday afternoon
House locked tighter than a drum
Eyes are stinging
Lungs are itching
Visibility declining
I'm in the suburbs
Hours from the nearest fire
The air conditioning keeps me cool
Tears flow for those at ground zero
The loss of life from human down
The loss of tree and grass
Homes and livelihoods lost
The air as thick as a Mallee dust storm
Damaged lungs that won't repair
Exhausted fighters on the edge of despair
These fires just keep on burning
Nightmare scenes of endless carnage
Screams of wildlife too slow to run
They've never seen the like before
But know that this is how it is to be
The end will come but who knows when
The land eventually will recover
But it will never be the same
It will never feel the same

This time will be given a name
As we did with Black Saturday
And Black Friday
The day the whole world mourned
When it seemed the whole of Australia burned.

Steve Boyce

The thought

of watching the inferno,
interminably, by myself

not having
had a dear friend's
condition to worry about

'The animals',
he sobbed in my arms,
back from Emergency, with
the forests burning on every channel

Jeltje Fanoy

Her bush un-settlement

Her sunburnt shores across the land
Overnight turn lush viridian leaves
To blackened ash;
Under blood-red skies
Apocalyptic cries ring out
Against the fiery monster
And blue-grey clouds conjure
Distorted biblical face
Billowing smoke across bushland
Leaving behind no trace of life
But for the Mallacoota birds, who squawk
The songs of new refugees in flight
Over ashen ruins
And the drought drinks up
Every drop of pitiful rain
And kangaroos bounce
Through burning flames of gold
Fuelled by gusty wind nights
And burning day suns –
And the sky above suffocates
In want of earthly rains
Fire breathes death to all living things
Merciless, in its path;
And there lies catastrophe
Upon the morn
A smouldering, still life portrait –
Her Australian face cindered
Her landscape torched
Upon her dusty earthen floor
She burns and weeps
Too dead to breathe

In her bush un-settlement
Aboriginal murmurs chant
Back-to-back in their rain dance
Cry heavenly tears upon the land
To heal her burning by God's hand
While good firefighters slay the beast
Wrestle snakes that hiss and spit
Thousands of gallons
At this wild inferno
Tango beast, red flared skirts rise to soaring heights
While we pray and await
Yellow armoured, heat proof souls —
For the cooling that never comes.

Susan Wakefield

Fire

I stand like a statue
in a big empty house.

Solitary, still: I ignite.

The house burns.

These words are my ashes.

Gayelene Carbis

Goodbye cruel world

these fires smack home
like a suicide note

mother's last words –
loved us, but leaving us

can't live with us –

any longer

Lance Convey

Unless water kills

A fire starts in a hollow log
or leaves in a branch, so hot
suddenly that creatures flee
who know enough of heat
they've heard it all before
I ask if you're in danger, you say
not red like a Rothko painting
won't stop here unless water kills
that fire log, which you say is
sucked away from passion
or cleverness, exploded
out of carelessness, now
utes loaded up with stuff
spare the home and shed
burn off the fear, courage
for the days that follow, heave
in smoke, what frankly is no more
look back on, then disappear.

Rob Schackne

Silvam incendit

Then vast fires grew, but not by roots, they
Took the crowns. Tree tops blazed as if vanquished
Kings on pyres were what they held aloft
Instead of leaves. But burning kings hold sway
In such a little space… these flames spread thick
And moved as if they were alive. Some scoffed
When we spoke of them jumping the river,
Until they did. Embers leapt from tree to
Tree, bright orange sparks in the thick smoke that
Engulfed the bush, paddocks, us. Wherever
The fire went, the heavy smoke pursued
It, curled into it, laid heavy ash at
Its feet as offerings. The crowns of trees
Burnt away like bright islands in grey seas.

Juleigh Howard-Hobson

Currowan fire (the fourth time around)

I see the storm in the fire.
In the heart of billowing black
a white bolt of lightning flashes
to a clap of thunder
igniting a wall of flames.

The beast rises over the ridgeline,
to the northeast
a wind gust away
from the last of the green treetops
surrounding our house.

So close to dry crackling grass
and wooden verandah
where I timorously keep watch
fire hoses uncoiled
ready the fourth time around

until the roar of the southerly change
rips the fire-front northward
racing up gullies and hillsides
consuming all in its path.

Dorothy Swoope

The Currowan fire began on 26 November 2019 in a climate of low humidity, high temperatures and baked, dry soil. Fanned by a west-north-westerly 'foehn' wind, fire spread rapidly; half a million hectares were-burned and hundreds of properties destroyed.

Dawn of fire

Fire breathes its hot breath,
takes and destroys. Skin burns

Like molten wax, scars and deforms,
When did we first imagine fire?

Its leaping strength;
When did we first tame it?

When did the first flames lie down,
burn into embers, to warm us?

We cherished its secrets. Held its
power in our hands, but whipped

our fingers out of reach.
I prod and poke, teasing

with another log. Spreading
warmth onto chilled skin.

Back in its crackling,
glowing, elemental beauty.

When did fire first become
our enemy?

Splinter of glass hidden
in hot grass. Red flames

on the hill. Scorching
heat. Ravenous tongues.

Eating everything in their path.
Spitting ash, everywhere.

Careless candle, caught by
gusts of wind. Suddenly

friend is foe. Greedy mouth,
foul black breath.

And ashes to ashes, in places
high and low, praise

the mystery behind the light.
Fire, friend and foe. Its

hypnotic glow flickers,
dies like fallen starlight.

Fire, fire, burn bright!
Dance across the dawn light.

Kathleen Panettieri

Waiting to rescue

You are distressed by the sight of creatures
fleeing for their lives and you cry for those
who do not make it. You want to help, donate
more than you can afford, but you have no conception
of the agony of those who wait and wait and wait

for *access to the fireground* where ringtails,
pygmy possums and gliders have all been incinerated:
where burned brushtails slumped in ash
long for the release of death and survivors in hiding
dare not venture out into the wasteland.

You who give and give and want humanitarian results
do not understand that, waiting on *access to the
    fireground*,
we are weeping because the burnt feet of macropods
will break down in a matter of days without treatment,
while echidnas and surviving birds are dying of thirst.

You do not know the drain, the soul-destroying agony
of waiting while the fire ground is cleared for entry,
the exhaustion of meeting the need when entry is gained
and the horror of having another fireground cleared
for entry when you have no more manpower to meet the
    need.

Jane Baker

Orange moons

Bushfires in the high country
burn for six and a half weeks
worry and waiting
smoke and heat
ash on the roses
blood red suns
orange moons
magpies breathless
longing for rain.

Fire map meetings
leave or stay
photographs in the boot of the car
grandfather's bible
grandmother's jade beads
mops and buckets
stuffed downpipes
phone trees, ember attacks
containment lines
hazard reduction
watch and act
fire crews with slip-ons
a new vocabulary.

Robin Purdey

Hi-Viz heroes

We're just your average Aussies, ordinary folk
On uneventful days we're the waste collection bloke
The lass who cuts your hair, a farmer, or a guard
Your dentist, or a sparky, the guy who mows your yard
Some of us live in the bush, others in the towns
Some have quarter acre blocks, and some extensive grounds
But when that pager beeps our diff'rent lifestyles cease to count
'Cause when we pull the Hi-Viz on your safety's paramount

We then become your first-responders, or their back-up crew
We put our hands up for the worst and pledge to see it through
To warn you of emergency we may go door-to-door
But sadly, sometimes not all folks can be accounted for
We'll cut you from a car wreck, or sandbag flooded creeks
We battle blazes 'cross the land which burn for weeks and weeks
We'll search the local bushland for a child who is lost
And we don't quit in spite of heat, or hailstorm or frost

We wear the colours of our kind, states vary in their hue
Protective gear to keep us safe while we're supporting you
Some of us will face the most confronting tasks of all
And have to live our lives out prayin' we made the right call
A few of us may never don the uniform again
Once we've had that first-hand look at families in pain
But we're no lesser for our lot, our hearts are no less true
We worked beside our colleagues and we did our best for you

And whether paid or unpaid, we are equal to the task
For when you need our services you only have to ask
And when the call comes in that my community's in danger
I won't care if you're my best mate or total bloody stranger
I'll still fight for your right to live, to save you if I can
An' you'll still call me 'hero' and you'll want to shake my hand
But that's not why I do the job, I don't need a citation
I'm the understated Hi-Viz type who's true to my vocation.

Sam Middleton

Volunteer firefighter

Australia is at war with bloody red flames
burning our land until charcoal remains

Volunteer firefighters - heroes of hope
Risk their lives through billowing smoke

Through the crackling intensity and dreadful smell
Their eyes are straining as they push through hell

Pausing momentarily and gazing around
seeing wildlife perishing – ash to the ground

They know our fauna will never be the same
As traumatised animals whimper with pain

The fighters may grab their water to share
with a wounded koala in a state of despair

Shattered, the fighters stare up in vain
Willing the heavens to send down rain

Though weariness shows on each blackened face
They won't allow fatigue to slow down their pace

Julie Annette King, Wanneroo

As mates

The swirling tips like licking lips
A localised apocalypse
All-consuming
Death is looming
And people try to come to grips

A devastating wall of flame
That's searching for more life to claim
A deadly dance
So little chance
It's hell by any other name

A vessel of annihilation
Instigating desperation
No matter fates
We'll fight as mates
And stand together as a nation.

Jai Thoolen

Facing the beast

Into the fray, with courage supporting our shoulders
Nozzles held hard, pointing at the beast
We fight a wall of fire, its burning breath heating our faces
The scorching heat travels down into our throats
Gulping air and smoke and ash, we hold our stance
A strange darkness shadows the daylight
We fight on, hearing the crackling shriek of trees ablaze
Living things leap by us not daring to stop
Flames lap at their tails as they escape
The hungry beast blackens the creatures not fast enough to flee
We wipe our tears of sweat away, holding our nozzles tight
Point our hoses at the beast and fight on.

Vacen Taylor

Fire this time

Casual conversation outside the pool
a fellow swimmer buttons her jacket tight
'Rain later, and that wind's rising.'
The Fife clouds are Persian cat grey
fluffy and anodyne, bearing showers.

But Australia, my mother's birthplace,
is orange with flame; People, animals
and townships perish. A fearful exodus
to the sea is underway.

It was the flood last time, Noah escaping
with the makings of life, two by two.
This time, fire will consume.

Slow, thick anger and shame rises:
we increased the earth's heat,
saw ice caps melt and fires rage
watched floods destroy homes.
We mocked the warnings.

Our primitive instincts activated
and reason suppressed, we pray
to the rain gods to alter course.
Take Scotland's rain, pour it
swift and sure, in healing cascades
Down Under.

Linda K. Menzies

Blue Mountains (Leura), 2019/20

Spring 2019

We wait for the Gospers Mountains fire to reach us.
At the RFS briefing we are told that this is new.
That this fire is not behaving like a normal fire,
that everything is burning,
that creeks aren't running,
that it was a matter of when, not if.

Every day we wake to smoke.
Clothes in cupboards smelt of it.
Food starts to taste of ash.

December 2019

The Bell's Line of Road becomes the front line.
We pour over maps and internet applications.
Car packed, we look through the smoke to the north
and go inside for coffee.

Thirty minutes later we go outside
to find burnt leaves falling from the sky
and a mushroom cloud of smoke over Mount Tomah.
That night we watch the flames light the sky.

January 2020

Just over the first hill
where the fire passed over the road
there is a sudden line of cars and people standing
silently looking to horizon of ash.

Our feet crush burnt branches
we smell the fire still fresh
an absence of birdsong
trees crumble in the breeze.

It is hard to read this country now
a charcoal ash poem
that stretches into the future.

Mark Roberts

* these verses are excerpts from a longer poem

48° C

Forty kilometres north,
ten thousand bats air-dry,
drop corpses on a pyre.

Here by the gate, a hare,
ears edged with ebony, fleet
harbinger of mourning.

Angus cattle, with the hide
of denialists, still
graze in the midday sun.

Silent in the swelter,
scarlet parrots wilt
on cane chairs, droop

on paths, emerald wings
ajar, floored by the heat,
mouths gape in the smoky air.

Forty kilometres south,
seven times the size of Singapore*,
the monster billows.

Brenda Proudfoot

---

* The Gospers Mountain 'mega fire' started from a single ignition point. It has now destroyed an area 'seven times the size of Singapore' (*Sydney Morning Herald*, 20 December 2019).

Sentinel

Solitary in the ashen hollow

black and charred
a burnt-out house

only the chimney remains

Threaded with desolate beauty
the fabric of its handmade
presence hovers

traces of smoke inhaled

Further away –
murmuring with anticipation
twined through rough stubble

voices in the void
turn into something else

Darrell Coggins

Climate revolt

the fires of summer came early & we've been taken hostage by
strangeness   on these days
of perpetual haze   enshrouded
while all still alive   & surely it's not our sun
this poisonous pink glow
that's taken control of the sky

                not a disgrace
                      to walk along the street
                            with a mask over your face –
                                you're not a surgeon
                                      nor a terrorist

 just need protection
        from these hazardous days
                while the state
                        burns itself to bits

the Rural Fire Commissioner's sad face on
   nightly tv
                'it's not going to be
                          the same
                              as it was before'

ambulances & fire engines panic down the street
sirens devour the air *earth has not anything to show*
less fair woman stacking tins at the grocery store
   can't stop coughing
girl at traffic lights white scarf covers her mouth
old man at the surgery says 'such a red sun
the end of the world' *dearest god*
when will I die

car headlights search their way

in the middle of the day
Australian flag   on the flagpole
falls utterly fatigued   misty towers
of the CBD   ghostly fade   from
a fantasy film

and everywhere the smell of conflagration
      breathing problems
         for those at risk

           CLOSE WINDOWS
           CLOSE CURTAINS
           CLOSE ALL GAPS

out in the country   someone is weeping
'everything's gone   there's nothing'
piece of ragged cloth   ablaze in the wind
'couldn't afford the insurance things just
got on top of us' kangaroos defenceless
in a blackened paddock   people hug each
other on an empty road near a burnt-out
car a family stand stunned outside the
carcass of their house   corrugated iron
no longer a roof fanned out oblique
like an art installation   'the really scary
moment when the sky went dark'
my life runs away continually

Carolyn Gerrish

Bushfire haiku

bushfire smoke
the blood red sun
sets the river alight

hot north wind - at the edges
clouds and tempers fray
white cockatoos swirl

uphill
an echidna searches blindly for ants
nose down

drought and heat
matriarch eucalypt
sheds her bark

sheep trapped, dumbfounded
in the corner of a paddock
wool on fire

fire evacuee
grandmother's pet cockatoo
set free but no escape

homeless
wearing stranger's pyjamas
sleeping in a strange bed

two hundred neighbours
a little weatherboard hall
fire update meetings

ashen ground
burnt forest – bare tree trunks
throw black shadows

mountains on fire
a farmer's gate
closed

eerie gold light
pink Cecil Brunner roses
orange by mistake

open beak
a breathless magpie gasps
where are the worms?

bushfire flames
heading up the road
ignore the 100k speed limit

drenching rain after bushfire
the river rushes downstream
ash grey

Robin Purdey

I love a sunburnt country

When Dorothea Mackellar famously penned
'I love a sunburnt country of droughts and flooding rains'
No one imagined the rains would stop
The droughts would flood
And the country would burn by the sun
My country is ablaze
Fires of astronomic proportion,
They can literally be seen from space
And just as glacial whites become one
With oceans of blue
Our famous red centre selfishly sweeps the nation Replacing its palette with a monochrome death

We politicise this tragedy with the left
Screaming climate change
The right screaming environmental mismanagement
And those stuck in the middle, simply screaming
Terror filled and terrified
They are forced from their homes
Drowning in the flames
Scrambling for existence
We argue which side of the fence we sit on
Forgetting just how grateful we should be
To still have a fence

Where once our prime minister brandished a lump of coal in parliament and arrogantly proclaimed 'This is coal, don't be afraid', he now backpedals on persuasion
Rhetoric fills the air as thick as the smoke itself
With both of them equally hard to swallow

Only one so glaringly transparent
Federal blames state, state blames federal
In a war of jurisdiction and boundaries

Meanwhile a scorching tsunami
Surges against the horizon
Crossing borders like those who seek asylum
Hectic and homeless.
And despite this, the war is fought by volunteers
Submerged in ash
Where those on the frontline
Bravely draw their battle lines
and some heroically flatline

28 dead, 2000 homes and 1 billion animals lost.
I can't help but draw comparisons to Notre Dame
An 850-year-old cathedral burnt to the ground and a billion dollars
rolled in before the flames were at bay.
Our country, our home, our land has been a place of worship for 80
thousand years
30 million acres of sacred site torched

I say fix this church
Because like Dorothea Mackellar,
We all love our sunburnt country
But we must act now
Before out of site becomes out of time

Niel Smith

Work clothes

Fires burn
you stand
in your work clothes
that is all you have
everything else is ash
now becoming sludge
as the rains come
not a blessing
for you stand
in your work clothes
there is work to do
although – not yet
nothing provides work
where destruction is total
scratching the earth
in crazed and broken frenzy
in a fury
in a heartache
to look to a new start
to repair
but there is no repair
only the taking of the
giant rake of survival
and to wait for help to come

they come
they see you standing there
in your work clothes
assume you are ready
to help
but your paralysis

is shock
that they are crying
and like the rain
which sprinkled
as an aftermath
it is not enough

you ask
can I have fresh work clothes

Patricia O'Gready

Gnangara fires

The horses know before we do.
Something soft, cloying and salt
on the air, stirring nostrils moon-ring
broad, a rattling inhalation.

Next, we hear the groan
turning over the paddocks.
The air creeps, then runs,
heat rising in spoiled milk curls.

The pines lean in as the wind browns.
Surrounded, cut and dried. Checking waters,
I can hear the kangaroos
bursting through the brush –

neat grey ghosts heading north,
hear the manic call of emu
shattering heated silence.
The horses spin, stuttered in pens.

There's always a plan
at the back of my mind
but the reality is slower,
shocked calm makes me walk

between the sheds
count the buckets and ropes,
prep the float, move the hay
but know in numb certainty

we cannot move it all.
But there's no fire here
for now. We wait in clumps
watch the horizon sink to red.

One friend was stopped
as the roads closed, her messages
pop and snap on my phone.
We are fine, so far

but pinned between decisions.
One friend is leaving, she cannot bear
to wait it out. Another has snuck
their four-wheel drive through the barrier

is slogging through the pines
to get to us. We shake heads
but cannot say out loud
we would not have done the same.

My black mare stands in the smoke,
has been here many times before.
Each helicopter dive turns an ear,
but she watches the trees first

as I stand at her shoulder. Her life
is marginal, introduced species
facing the oldest trauma – unwelcome
stowaway within the storm.

This time, we are lucky. Flames roll back,
subside to sand. The pines stretch new scars,
quiver scorched limbs. The horses
lower their heads. The parrots do not return.

Siobhan Hodge

It didn't start this way

air thick with acrid smoke
distorting the skyline
people's living rooms now dust
schools where the future is buried
workplaces where livelihoods have perished
bushland burning a red and orange inferno

the dystopian novels I read
the fiction they portray
they didn't start off this way
the sun didn't suddenly disappear one day
they start this way
permafrost thawing
long droughts
extreme heat
government policies
special interests and profits
uncontrolled fires

they creep up on us
when we are deaf to expert advice
a neglect of our earth begins
a denial of the facts persists

today I'm not reading a dystopian novel
but prefacing a historical account

Mary Chydiriotis

Air purifier

It started and it did not stop. The fatigue was hard to explain. The first days were a novelty. It rolled in like fog. It wasn't campfire smoke. It didn't evoke memories of friends, of country parties or beach barbecues. It smelled of old, dead smoke that turned to crust in the lungs.

And it lingered. It clung to hair, to car seats. It burrowed into our clothes and forced its way into our skin. We kept hearing, 'Unprecedented.' It looked like winter but it felt like summer. The feeling didn't match the view. So many things were out of order. The streets were empty, subdued like in mourning. The sounds of summer should have been there, lazing around the oceanless valley like a welcome holiday visitor, lying across each other like a family on a lounge in front of the single blast from the fan. There was just the slow roll of the tram, pushing through the smoke with its headlights on at midday.

The smoke that came was from flame that took and took. The smoke that came was sharp and burnt lungs and throats. The smoke that came had chewed up so much. It stole the summer and all its celebrations. It put down glasses. How can we celebrate? How can we dance in the smoke while our neighbours stand in the ashes of their lives?

KL Morris

Evacuation

As the darkness settled in, we could see the orange glow,
Flickering bright then muted, from about three k's below.

Checking all the socials, before we all lay down to rest,
The warnings said to 'watch and wait' while the firies did their best.

Waking with a jolt, confusion pushed away my dreams,
The sound of blaring sirens, and my awake and yelling teens,

A megaphone announcing from the chopper in the cloud,
'RESIDENTS OF FREEMANS ROAD YOU MUST EVACUATE NOW!'

My mind snapped straight to clear, and we all leapt up to act,
It was 3 am, we ran outside to see how the fire had tracked.

The flames flickered on the horizon, about one kilometre away,
The police were at the door, saying that we couldn't stay.
My partner hitched the float up to the car, in a frantic hurry,
But it could only take two horses, and we had five, which was the worry.

The only way out by car was down the mountain road,
So with the old horse and the young horse on, carefully he towed.
The fire burning roadside, and in the treetops overhead,
Driving through the smoke and heat, as flames and embers shed.

My eldest daughter took a car, a dog and a few possessions,
Disappearing bravely down the road to join the fleeing processions.
That left myself and my youngest daughter, behind on the mountain top,
With three horses and no vehicles, we waited and we watched.

My husband called us, panicked – the firemen would not let him come back,
I said if it got worse, we'd ride them down the mountain track.
Hellfire Pass, that daunting trail, is a long and rocky vertical drop,
If the fire jumped the road, we would be trapped up at the top.

We saddled up the horses and we watched the flames approach,
My mobile phone was ringing, it was the sergeant with reproach.
He told us it was time to leave and onto our mounts we swung,
Riding one and leading one, the smoke filling our lungs.

Into the bush we vanished, hooves sliding down that treacherous pass,
An eerie stillness filled the scrub, nothing stirring in the grass.
An hour passed and we were down, safe at the mountain bottom,
A frightening experience that would never be forgotten.
We stayed that night at public yards, with all our furry friends,
When it was safe to return, we saw how close that it had been.

We are so very thankful for all our emergency services,
In times of greatest need, they certainly don't desert us.

Kirily Isherwood

Devastation 2020

How to convey the numbness I feel
watching footage of flames racing
through forested mountains and towns,
of scorched cattle and wildlife fleeing in terror,
of a sky now orange now red now greyish black
the ash-filled smoke choking the landscape,
of roads snaked with cars of families evacuating
of house after house burned to the ground.

How can I presume to write as a woman
staring at the twisted remains of her house
cherished dreams and mementos lost in the ashes,
who wipes wet cheeks and soot-rimmed eyes
turns to the camera and says it's all gone
but somehow we'll start again.

How can I presume to write as a farmer
gazing in anguish at his charred land and stock
all his feed and sheds lost in the blaze,
who with red-rimmed eyes faces the camera
and says it's all gone
but somehow we'll start again.

How can I presume to write as one of the firefighters
exhausted from battling flames month after month
or as a volunteer or emergency worker
or as one of the trapped or one of the fleeing
or a family member of the missing or dead?

I am not there, not there among them
I pray for their safety
I think of the present here in this country
I think of the future facing this planet

I am numb

Lilian Cohen

Tanka

blackened waves
lap charcoal beaches …
who are the keepers
of sandcastle dreams
for our children

Barling's Beach, February 2020

Michelle Brock

ice fire stone

I shall wear no more ice
the cloak is slipping from my shoulders
and will swell the rising seas
I shall wear no more ice   only fire

in my cloak of rising water
I see those who must flee   go to war
for a dry place to stand
I shall wear only rock and rising water

my cloak it is fire and stone
you drilled and you have mined me
you frack and refine me
now my cloak it is fire and stone

Nick Allen

How to protect the lungs

Inhalation of ash is the new normal
as I fashion myself Jungian,
transpersonal, still able to scribble and scrawl
what dreams are left to me,
while my hands wrinkle and curl to crone,
and the forest burns. All forest,
not just this one here by the garden.
I'd watch and wait, evacuate,
but it's far too late for that now.
Instead, I code the Pantone:
666-Apocalypse, this iron-red sky at noon.
The great age of the Millennial,
no longer dirty thirties cruising the Apps —
we've merged into Millenarian.
Self-flagellants in the suburbs in the smoke,
backs beaten raw with single-use plastic guilt,
upcycling fails;
the cold congeal of a non-free-range
drive-thru breakfast.
Down at the oval there's a ghost-dance or cargo-cult —
ascension by meditation in tool sheds
disguised as spaceships,
or could it be the other way around.
I gather with the rest of them on rooftops at dawn,
waiting for whatever comes next,
howling out the absurdity of all school bells now
the soup-sky of dust and bone-bits and burnt leaves
has clogged up lungs until the voice is a raw cough —
and then silence. It has come to this.
There's a netherworld waiting, just beyond
these prophetic dreams I've almost

stopped mapping out.
A collective unconscious of underground angels
granting passage through
fire-fuelled cognitive dissonance,
offering ascension through ash and mire
and on out the door
as though future fields could feel green,
as though the heavens could ever again know
Yves Klein blue.
But like stars above air pollution,
future fantasy feels extinct.
In deepest sorrow, I fashion myself practical,
line up to buy a box of masks from Bunnings.
The serious kind.

Ivy Ireland

Koala in flight from bushfire

Buddha
in the fork of a gum
joey blind
to the crimsoned sun
to the bronze-coloured haze,
the palpable air – litter of black
leaf, twig

with redonned eyes
she turns her gaze
from the
turbulent skies
to the top of the trunk,
ascends,
meditates;
& makes a quick descent
to flee

the gum
at one
with Bodhi tree

Barbara Petrie

rigor mortis

a rigor mortis of black grass
like burned spines of a dead animal
remains of ravaging fire

on the map a black Rorschach blob
read: climate change

carrion swoop on exposed animals
ferals travel to burnt out spots

rivers are not safe
fish dying from ash poisoning

a rigor mortis of politics
burnt out minds from too much coal
not thinking: climate change

Susan Hawthorne

Thirteen ways of sighing in an ecocide

After Wallace Stevens

Waves sigh and crumble
at Newport Beach. Phantasms of mist
twist off like smoke won't.

    On a soft-sand jog
    I bury four cormorants, lift them
    on driftwood where grains spin and sigh.

Worsening news and a worsening sky.
I can't tell if it sighs.
The wind dies, is death.

    Twilight from three
    is one kind of future (and sigh).
    Sunnies on, each again.

North Sydney's Cloud City
from *The Empire Strikes Back*;
I feel its captive carbon sighs
climb my eery skin.

    Tomato vines sag and sigh,
    won't fruit, choke
    like outdoor children.

We sigh and accept
the sun is the moon in this
taming of us –
mask reversed, a frantic air.

    The PM's office denies
    he's in Hawaii, sighs

It's not a story. Nice try.

My New Year's dream
beside a blood-red feed:
a sphere crowned by haze
in the sigh of space
relies on us more than we do.

    Remind me now
    how love confounds the powerful.
    Sighs carry accents,
    a stroke of your hair.

A billion lives? No sigh on earth
exists for this. For insects, countless.
Save one without end.

    A silver morning's soundless sigh.
    Could azure breach
    October's strikes, shadow and light
    sit apart at funerals?

A sigh of rain no minor godsend,
but some old frogs sing.
When this Summer's buried,
I must warn the cormorants
under the sand or clear sky
it rests with them.

Toby Davidson

Fire through the screens

We are taken back to basics,
ashen-faced creepings
on the fringes of survival.

We cannot count the sheep,
melted down to fibres,
pulped thousands, tonnage down.

Swaddled koalas, possums netted
in helmets, carried to cool creche
where the funds don't always reach.

There's no justice caught in the branches,
stretching limbs to red-dirt moon
cowering beneath the smoke,

the towers are growing, pipped
as rain falls short, too thin for cover.
We cannot stop the clock.

Another few seconds, midnight sun
rises upon the fallen rooftops,
bared crowns peeling in the heat.

We cannot turn the tide, pull air back
to cooked lungs. Each small step
is filtration, minnows over stones.

Bushfire mounts the coast, bearing down
the numbers. We will weigh these costs
in minerals more precious than oil.

Shattered dam lines, we are blitzed
and battered, watching behind screens
no thicker than our breath.

When relief comes, it is cold shock
drawn out and through. Too many limbs
to soak the fall, arched and burning

a dead sea, strangled desert memorial
of lakes in flames. The smell of singeing hair
caught in our lenses, mirroring on and on.

Siobhan Hodge

White peaches

Word went around Moruya –
six crates of white peaches –
saved from Jack's Araluen orchard.
'This is the last of them,' Jack said
'there won't be any more. Once gone,
gone. Every peach tree in my orchard
burned to the ground.'
How many can we eat before they disappear?

Moya Pacey

Leaving Canberra

We are leaving Canberra. Going inland, from air that
 chokes
more than smoke from the steam trains of our childhood
 days.
Our bags are jam-packed with items from a list
found on Emergency Fire Survival Kit.
Families have instructions and boxes of P2 masks
should they evacuate quickly if fires move their way.
They have hand-written details for finding the hidden key
of our rustic country cottage in case we're on a walk.

The sky will be blue, air clearer. My lungs will cease to
 sting.
Bees will hover over the calendulas' apothecaries.
I will open the windows, hear magpies' clarinets
and cockatoos' bad language as they prune the trees.

We have checked *Fires Near Me*. Found the roads are clear.
Now I feel that I'm deserting everybody here.

Hazel Hall

A new normal

North Leura, 15 December 2019. Looking north, watching Mt Tomah burn.

Smoke seeps through walls
we wake to gardens covered in ash
burnt forests carried high
on wind gusts   a sacrifice
you don't understand
and so will be repeated.

Sun dimmed in afternoon haze
a black circle around party pink
fading to a defeated grey.

Over the ridge new weather patterns are
being invented. Sheets of flames swirl
into cones, billowing clouds dark with fire
throw lightning bolts at fire trucks.

Wait for the wind to change
decide whether to head east or west.

Mark Roberts

Sunshine Coast to Sydney, January 2020

When the end of the world comes
I think it will be like this: a storm of flame
and wind, eucalyptus burning. Sinking
to our knees will do no good. Kangaroos,
children, even flying foxes will not be nifty
enough to get away. As for planes still in the air,
will passengers grasp what's happening?
Will they drop their G & T's and rush to stare
at the earth's incandescent terrain? Will they
lament the black sky, volcanoes, mountains
of flame? Will they show remorse? Will they
utter words like '*Biblical*', '*Apocalypse*'?

Or will it be like this, Flight JQ 791,
Sunshine Coast to Sydney, where I peer
through scratched plexiglass to thick smoke
30,000 feet below: bushfires raging. I want
to shout, grieve, but my neighbours flip through
glossy magazines, order more bling.
Why are we not standing in the aisle, keening?
Have we forgotten they're part of us –
those legs running nowhere, that singed fur,
thousands of wings beating faster,
the koalas, lizards, bees trapped in hives –
they are *us*, they are *ours*, those lost lives.

Rosie Jackson

Wildfire

This holiday of ordinary things in the shooting gallery
flung side to side evading the mistimed bullets of misfortune
on a day that sears beyond hot with a wind to strip out the last drop
as the grass cracks and ignites to race a raging cackle
and spread a black smudge in its wake.

The orange tease tricks its way up tree trunks
flicks its frenzied laugh through the treetops
to erupt scrub and leaves bright and loud.

Mercury slugs higher than it should and men and women
in heavy fluro jab rakes and hoses at the advancing edge
a heeler nipping the heels of a mob shifting, nudging
the mass ever so slight, pulling 12-hour shifts
under the whup whup of water bombers and news choppers.

How easily the treasures of man erupt in red and orange
to a remnant of tangled steel and ash as 57 homes
and one life are chalked on the board,

In a land with fire as its heritage there is an arrogant
    disrespect
from men who build without regard for the laws of fire
and stare incredulous when the news on television is in
    their yard.
When the misaimed gun fires in their face
with its burnt black residue.

Gary Colombo De Piazzi

Bushfire moon

fire watch
the first pulses
of the pager

summer night fire
all along the mountain
wild scars of red . . .
safe, she wipes the soot
from her baby's toes

emergency warning
wide-eyed horses
speckled with ash

bushfire sparks
on a shearwater's egg
ready to hatch

highland lake
burnt button-grass
on both sides of the moon

fatal wildfire . . .
cloud shapes explode
into crimson and black

no moon tonight
only burnt stars
and wattles in the breeze

summer heat
a currawong settles uneasy
in the jacaranda tree,
fire front embers
glow and twist through twilight

flames move faster
exploding into colours
orange and red,
adrenalin burnt in blackened eyes
the firefighter's deep tiredness

smoke and ash
flying tin angels
work the skyfall

days of firefighting
opening the window
to smell the rain

tired of this world
suddenly moonlight
through my window

end of shift
returning my name badge
to the pile.

Ron C. Moss

* excerpts from the book, *Bushfire Moon*

Part Three

AFTERMATH

'after the fire
the scent of not knowing
what the future holds'
   Tony Steven Williams

'The air smells of smoke, even after the rain.'
   Geoff Callard

'Smoke catches in the throat
settles deeper inside, a living part of us.'
   Brenda Saunders

Refugee

She saw the smoke turned black
it was like a childhood nightmare
tentacles that reached her
arms that choked and strangled
and then the fires sprouted
like wild mushrooms here, there
and everywhere, soon these became
violent flames which devoured
the undergrowth and climbed
the old gum trees like agile athletes
in seconds the canopies were alight
the unbearable noise resonated
like thunder in her ears and
her heart was an engine at full speed
she grabbed the suitcase which contained
the history of her life: letters, poems,
documents and photos and ran
she sped towards her car and
turned around for one last look
but instead closed her eyes
once safe in the car she asked herself:
Where now? … Where now?

Beatriz Copello

Post inferno

The day after evacuation, we're waiting at the base of the hill to return. At last, we're given the all-clear to drive with caution past the barrier and up the looping road ahead. As we ascend, the slope is still alive with smoulder, the occasional split and crack of eucalypt laid low. This burnt-toast smell will linger for weeks. Smoke shades the sun in a sombre midday twilight. Stubborn patches of red flame throb and incandesce on blackened trunks and branches. Sparks buzz, pop in multiple short circuits, their weird jigs flickering in our car windows. All those colours, shades, patterns, shapes – danger dressed in nightclub mode – it seems wrong to find beauty here, but we do.

Rounding the corner now, hoping, hoping that the familiar gabled roofline will be unbroken. Our home. Devastation if it's gone, such guilt if we're OK but those around us are wiped out . . .

after the fire
the scent of not knowing
what the future holds

Tony Steven Williams

No word

One time this scene was lush and green
One time the air was clear
One time I flew with those I knew
All through the bush land here
There was great sound from sky to ground
All chirp and croak and chatter
The smell was grand across this land
And nothing else could matter

This scene is black from front to back
The colour disappeared
No more the same since touched by flame
It feels eerie and weird
The smell of char comes from afar
I sit, a lonely bird*
Life will return after the burn
Today I have no word

David L. Flaxman

* sulfur crested cockatoo

City in smoke

I caught a train across the invisible bridge,
surrounded by the impenetrable fog.
I looked for my hometown
in menial tasks, dates kept, shopping done,
I drank coffee in 'boujee' cafes
while the majority of the continent was ablaze around me.
Bizarrely, life continued normally,
for me, or as normally as it could.
But ah, how my mind wandered
to the houses lost, the lives it cost,
the ashes of the country I was inhaling,
what I might do to be of use,
the futility of it, and the excuse
that nothing I could do mattered.
I hoped, at least
that those who might make a difference
realised then that they ought to have been trying.

I can't remember the last time the sky
was deep and unspoiled blue.
Is this new grey and yellow hue
the norm? What fiery form
will our summers take from here on in?
How many can Australia give before this sunburnt country
gives way completely beneath the weight
of its own disintegrated self?
The sun glowed red, the danger felt real,
even for me, a lucky one, a one who choked
in an unburnt house in an untouched city,
a city in smoke.

Erin Frances

sepia sky

the smoke slips
in through the cracks
chars the delicate green that
day after day   from the morning cuppa
to the last sip of the sun
was cultivated
with water   exercise   vitamin D
and visualisation

the colours and times of day
have disappeared
only the sepia sky
sprawls across the horizon
fills my lungs with the slow
burn of loss

Irina Frolova

In the valley of dying stars

'and when we breathe, that hollow rasp is Death'

The sky coughs blood,
her emphysemic lungs convulse in flame
and smoke the morning's light to black.
Though on this paltry plastic boat
our sodden forms grope together in pain,
I can feel the Earth, she's dying
and I hear her life dissolve in quiet rage.

Above that hill those deep embittered flames
lurch up to suck the sky's abyssal plane.
The final cracks of desperate life
fade quickly cross the dark and hollow lake.

There are those that sit and watch us burn.
They do not care to hear our mother scream,
as on her writhing corpse they rape
'til from her gouged collapsing gut
each piece of worthless gold is saved.

That rotten smell of death.
The blackened sun.
I do not dare to breathe
from ash corrupted lungs.

a bird may fly tomorrow.
Our hanged souls
should not.

Órlaith Ní Brádaigh

* Epitaph from Charles Baudelaire's 'To the reader' in *The Poems of Stanley Kunitz*, 1928-1978, trans. S Kunitz: Little, Brown and Company, Boston, 1979

Rescuing refugees

On Mallacoota Beach they huddle
women and children, dogs, some men
The sky lowers red
Blusterous winds cause havoc
Flames and waves lick
at opposite ends of the sand

The sky turns black with smoke
and burning embers fall
It seems like a slice of Bosch's Hell
The bushfire creating its own weather
pyrocumulus clouds cause lightning
Burning koalas shriek
Any escape by land is blocked

A luxury cruise ship heaves into sight
Its passengers have been told
to prepare to take on board
the scared and suffering refugees
holiday makers and locals together

The ship has exotic food
one butler per cabin
plenty of luxury room for all
But Canberra has decided it would look better
if the Army did the rescue
(The PM being badly in need of anything
that would make him look better)

The cruise ship turns majestically
leaving desperate refugees
still waiting on the sand
the flames roaring behind

the embers falling
Water close to keep them safe
as long as they don't drown
waiting for the Army's boats

Virginia Lowe

Aboard the Choules

From off the point we boarded
Children crying, sons and daughters
The beach still bore its eerie loneliness
The fire that seared it leaving many homeless

Upon a ship built to fight
A final spray from the salty mist
Steady motion into the abyss
Gave us a home for a day and a night

Bearing peace in the dark and hope in the light
Saving thousands off the smoky shore
Once aboard to be kindly told
'What's ours is yours'

Slowly the cold night fades
Daybreak reveals the warmth of the sun
HMAS Choules made of steel, sturdy and bold
Holds a crew with hearts of gold.

Alexandra Wallis, age 14

Australia visits Minnesota

There are two main types of snow,
one slices skin, pierces organs, pretends friendship and fun,
the other falls gently into submission, curls into the folds of embrace,
forms the smile to frame nostalgia.
I walk in snow to forget the other half of my face
staring at the blaze running towards the verandah.
This snow shares the air produced
by two nuclear plants,
5 million heaters and hearths,
a smoke snaking itself across the equator,
particles feel like grit in our teeth.
Coughing comes in cold and hot weather
it carries our conversations,
stalks our voices.

Angela Costi

* January 2020

Lithgow

I remember coming down the switchbacks into Lithgow
Couldn't see the road ahead because of the blizzard
Saw cars that had crashed and police warning signs
Cursed I'd bought a Holden in the blazing heat of summer
And hadn't noticed there was no heater in the vehicle.
Must have been mid-1970s, Whitlam was PM
And the world was exciting and full of hope,
We were young lived and loved on music and dope.

Now over the ridge comes a glow and ash flakes
Instead of snowflakes, can't see the road for smoke.
The wind is blowing towards us and an awful dread
Creeps through the town, yet still people have to live,
Help each other, do the mundane tasks and chores
Glancing over shoulders at the approaching inferno.
When you hang out the washing don't forget to blow
The ash away from the line where it sits like dirty snow.

Now in the words of Matt Trounce
Who witnessed it for himself:
It's here.
Ash and black leaves falling like rain.
Sirens everywhere.
It's hit the town on a few fronts.
We are packed but staying and watching at the moment.
Words of stoicism, grit and full of good intent.

We're still waiting, watching and waiting,
but the waiting may soon be over.
What more can I say (this probably means reams)

All words are written in fast-flowing streams
Whether on concrete, marble, paper or the net
They disappear on gravestones, in books and bytes
There are only jumbled pieces left when the fire hits,
Has passed through. A fireplace and twisted iron.
Yet the Government is unchanged, the PM denies
That mankind inflicted this, helped along by all the lies.

We're waiting, watching and waiting, waiting
for the crows to come home and the blame to fall
like the ash that permeates everything.
No blame for policies that pollute the earth,
because the backers are multinational despoilers
And open-cast mining brings wealth to a few
And jobs to some. But Australia is a country
That has sunlight enough to power the world,
Snowy mountains hydro schemes that produce
Electricity galore for all, and coastal wave power
For heating, lighting, aircon and the odd shower.

We're waiting, watching and waiting, waiting for …
For what? Perhaps an election when the wait is over.

Richard Soloway

Seven snapshots of the east coast fires

1.
The wind is relentless, dry.
Beyond the bay, above distant hills veiled in ethereal white,
thick grey clouds billow out across a clear blue horizon

smoking headlands
their silent beauty belies a dark reality.

2.
Watching from the beaches
in shared disbelief

with camera and phone we try to make real
the terrible import of what we are witnessing.

3.
Distance, like the vacuum of space
blocks the fearful roar
as unseen monsters devour land and life.

4.
Ancient rainforest
no longer immune to flame
awnless to this ravaging

Gondwana in ashes.

5.
Since the fires
I have not seen the black cockatoos.

I miss the cry that cuts the air
and echoes the pain in my heart.

6.
Last night
the northern sky glowed a most tender subtle pink.

This morning
three are dead, others missing, houses lost
and much woodland and wildlife gone.

7.
As the fire burned through the forest
toward the little green lake,
the water birds flew from their nests in the canopy
leaving behind their fat fluffy chicks.

As the fire died away . . .
translucent, glowing through the smoke haze,
we watched a perfect circle of reddish orange
drop slowly toward the horizon.

Amanda Stewart

Time of dying

Char cloys for days.
We stumble, crossing
uncounted acres of ash
and torched remains
following screams of the burnt.

We avert our gaze
from farmers' eyes
as bullets terminate the herd's pain,
and from the caring hands
filling decisive needles.

Oily smoke clouds
block the sun, drifting
beyond the horizon's edge
and the world knows
what our leaders deny.

Tiny shoots strive
to change the desolation.
Green ruptures layers of ash
and uncurling leaflets
grace ravaged stumps.

Still we scoff
at the ancient way
of understory burning,
practised long before our sails
dotted the horizon.

Marilyn Humbert

Firelife

Sky sucked dry
a smudge of pale taupe
a trace of blued steel
meets the blade of the horizon

above the heads of eucalypts
flutters of orange
netted in green

firestorms rear and sear
reflect in glass
shattered
on cindered paths

a creeping flame
bared skin

ash appliqués charred earth
a coverlet of black rain

Gail Willems

Functionality extinct

Mobile device pumping
radiofrequency radiation;
people listening to podcasts,
lectures about saving the planet,
transmissions streaming,
occupying Bluetooth headphones,
tuning out reality.
    No steps to address
    tech production chain mess –
    Nobody making the big call
    to reduce the
               carbon footprint.

Street artists spray messages,
decorating brick walls,
colourful phrases declaring
environmental outrage
dispensed from an aerosol can
packed with propellant.
    Chlorofluorocarbons, hydrocarbons,
      volatile organic compounds
        piercing the
                ozone layer.

Fire in the edifice belly
fuels humanitarian generosity,
generating a billion bucks;
donations destined to preserve history,
rebuilding the Paris drawcard of Notre Dame.
    Pity there was not a damn
      about rattling the tin can
      to tackle the
               garbage patch.

Embers in the wind,
remnants of forgotten forest fuel
filling nostrils with blackened blood –
on whose hands does the ash rest?
    We were once proud
    people of the land –
    Now the land has taken people
               in flames of retribution.

Shucking the mollusc
drowning in a pool of Worcester,
robbing the ocean of vital wild warriors
born to filter saltwater impurities
destined to prevent coastal erosion,
mass murdered along with the fish population,
under massive attack,
high demand aphrodisiac.
    Functionally extinct,
    no significant ecosystem role left to play –
    The world is not our
               oyster.

Kelly Van Nelson

Ash mounds

Softly powdered by rising ash
I walk towards a leaning
Stack of tin
There is no wind now to
Flail the trees
The bare blackened trees are silent
The birds have gone away
Or died

Here by the tin is a greater pile of ash
I don't know what this
Once was...
That sofa
Uncle Bob sat in
And would watch the cricket,
And Lillee off his long run?
Maybe a cupboard,
That one with the
Crockery that was the
Your mother's?
No, reckon it's the desk,
The old one,
The drawers crammed
With old photos,
Mementoes in matt and gloss
Old bikes,
Tom's mullet,
(Christ that mullet)
The twins so little
And some cousin no-one
Now remembers?

All gone.
The evidence of these pasts
Now reduced by the fire's
Wild erasing fury to
Mounds upon a landscape
White grey remains of a history
The ash will not tell

Geoffrey Bonwick

What's saved

Fruit bats fall dead from the trees
        magpies hurl their barren nests
Then cinders become our new black.
Carbonised leaves are the last filigree.

Cities burn.
The air is overcoat grey,
sometimes when bushfires are nearer,
                      shit-smeared apricot.
These two are the last colours left.

A spitting rain hits soil, there's no permeation…
runoff scribbles obituary all down towards the town drains.
Even fire lost interest as it rooted about
the debris that thinks it's forest floor.
Feathers hide in soot. Fur sits in dismal clumps
& this is no seasonal moult.

Saw Steve last week
    to know titans tire.
He's been most of season out of town
to a point where the land wears his sweat
& he carries the smoke home to his partner.
Peter says he loves the solitude
but misses his man's hands
when he's absent or just back, exhausted.

Woodchips are fashionable this year,
concrete paths don't burn
but occasionally I find something…

Les Wicks

Chimneys

All that remain
are chimneys.
Blackened brick statues
standing among the ashes.
Dark reminders of the need
for warmth
in winter.

How ironic
these smoke tunnels
survived
the deadly inferno.

A different winter came,
a manic frenzy,
raging, suffocating.
Nature devouring its own.

Helen Budge

How loss happens

The air smells of smoke, even after the rain.
We eat our fried rice; I pick out the lap cheong,
mum and dad talk about last weekend when we drove
to the country to a place owned by my Uncle's friend.
Hot winds, dusty roads, a farm full of citrus
blossoms and ostriches,
a family of six girls and one boy. I fell in love
with one of them at the dinner table but never said anything.
Their mother brought in plates
of sizzling lamb and potatoes roasted in fat
and I became a little bit more Aussie.

I am no longer a boy; scant memory of those early days
and that everyday family who embraced us,
until yesterday when I saw, on the
interactive map
of the fires, the name 'Bega
Valley', and I wondered
if they still lived there and if they
were ok. I called Uncle
and google-mapped their address
(from what we could remember)
but of course, everything looked normal.

Is this loss?
Not just the sudden wrenching away,
but the not knowing, the slowly forgetting.
Is it the hollow man in the white shirt
grasping for handshakes while my elderly
parents turn from the television
in shame and anger,
making me feel
just a little less Aussie?

Geoff Callard

Blue stain and silence

It's eerie,
this blue staining of asbestos sealant
on odd walls and clumps of shattered fibro
down both sides of the mountain street.
Nothing moves, nothing makes a sound
in this blackened landscape wreathed in blue.

A burned-out car, a child's trike melted into twist,
a bucket slumped to one side – these things you note
but the blue stain and silence get to you, and
you leave hurriedly, conscious of desecration –
these were the homes of your neighbours.

Jane Baker

Burning

Red-orange sky over the Sound this morning.
Here, it means rain – I wish they could have it.
There, it means something else.

Travelling back from the Shipwreck Coast
inland through wooded hills
we saw the effects: weird trees
where twigs of new foliage grew straight out
from blackened trunks like armless hands.
And there was one plant that needed fire –
sprang from scorched ground, bloomed best then.
In the Red Centre, too, among the desert oaks
and scrub, little black brushwood tangles.

But I never saw live fire. That tiny photo
he sent with the email was enough
to give a mother nightmares.
Sky entirely orange and opaque with smoke.
A road free from traffic but for a single
fire truck facing left. A tree in full leaf,
an expanse of buff dry grass. And on the truck
three tiny yellow heads. They're standing somehow
behind the cab (he's the one on the left, the shortest one)
and looking back to where a tidal wave of light
comes at them down the empty road.

Chris Considine

Burnt

Centre aisle sidle to window seat throne.
Outside, let the spinning begin, the air screws propel,
beam you upward and on through a clear blue domain,
way over the stretch marked parchment beneath
incoherently waiting for
waters to break.

The seat belt sign flicks on:
turbulence.

Click, brace. It flicks off. Unclick, unbrace.
Tap your phone, inflight news, inflight views.
Tea or coffee? Sip, and glance down from your throne:
same raw scuffed paddocks, same
Rorschach black bush.

Catch your breath, lean forward, look, see –
on the hillside, that scarlet slit,
that vulva ripped –
FIRE.
Like you see on the news, only real.
Only now.

Nero fiddles while Real burns

Dorothy Simmons

The old burnt gum

In quiet strips of what was left,
an old burnt gum stood black as coal
the embered flames had taken the grains
and the ancient trees left soul

The kookaburra flew the distance,
though he cried a wretched sound,
he did not laugh nor land once there,
he shrieked over sacred ground

Flying towards a safer place,
he was in sorrow against the sky
the fires burnt below his wings,
he would surely die

He found by heart direction
away from the ravaged land of smoke,
he shrieked in the lonely language
as if by soul he spoke

'My gumtree full of laughter,
to ash and dust the plains,
all because of stupid humans lighting fires,
they have no brains'

He flew away in sounds of angst
against the spirited light,
and as the sun went down in amber
a blaze below, had sung goodnight.

Nardine Sanderson

Smoke

For weeks now the gauze sky stretches white
holds the smell of fire. Lost in the haze
streets are strangely silent. There is no wind.
Day and night our houses fill with smoke.
It searches for cracks, gaps in the skirting.
Doors once open to a summer breeze barred
against it. Everywhere, a hint of gum leaves
lingers, the scent of a campfire trapped indoors.
Blackened embers line our windowsills.
Unseen, lighter than air, the distant fire floats
freely among us. Every breath leaves us
light-headed. Smoke catches in the throat
settles deeper inside, a living part of us.

Brenda Saunders

Sturdy bodies

three of the garden gnomes survived
faces smeared with soot
jackets and hoods seared scorched
splattered with fire hose jets

sat mourning their brethren
not so lucky non-Irish gnomes
one toppled and headless
exposing a *Made in China* sticker

pressed hard against the ground
on his base through the fires
the gold label shines bright as the day
it was thumbed there in China

these survivors haven't much of a garden
shrubbery topiaried by flames
silhouetted skeletons and wrack
the horizon now the hedge is gone

they'll sit tight with all they survey
until new windows reflect their sturdy
bodies and perky hoods
unlike the old window panes

pooled in glassy tears
beside the rubble

Jane Downing

Ash

The memory is like burnt toast,
the smell lingers too long,
in my kitchen, in my house,
seeps into the curtains.
And I don't know what to do to cauterise
this lingering, except to open the curtains,
the blinds, the windows, watch the light filter
through the remnants of ash on the glass,
a film of chalky makeup on its face.

But this play has gone on too long,
the natural light reveals what the stage light
could not; the actor is not happy.
A finger swiped across the outside window
leaves a smear of clarity,
pink skin exposed to oxygen.
Her vision is no longer frosted,
Medea's mask melts
like cheap foundation in the heat.

The actor is not happy, and she knows
the role she must now play
when she exits stage right.
The dress rehearsal is over
and toast is burning in the kitchen.

Natalie D-Napoleon

Possum requiem: Ode to Mallacoota

The phone rang.
He told us we had lost our home:
'I've been for a drive, I'm still alive.
My home is gone and so is yours.'
Engulfed in flames
on New Year's Eve.
Just too hard to believe...
How do I say goodbye
to our ancient tree
that held so many birds
safe in its arms?
How do I say goodbye to
a koala, our koala: Aristotle,
sheltered in its crook?
The birds. Our birds!
A glimpse of golden light
in the western sky,
and then
gelato colours,
softest pinks and blues,
Mallacoota hues...
fading to dark
revealing glittering stars
above Mallacoota waves,
on the cool night balcony
the salt air wrapping its gentle breezes
around us and caressing our souls...
How do I say goodbye to
a night-time visit from our possum friend,
who gave us possum hugs... Is he alive? Did he survive?
My heart beats in time with

this forest and this sea.
How can it be
that I must say goodbye
to this paradise?
I can always buy a new toaster,

a kettle, a cup, a plate,
but it's too late, too late
to sit together on our old blue couch, on our verandah,
and watch the rainbow lorikeets
frolic, or Mrs Magpie sing for her supper,
or play guitar in the morning sun…
and music with friends on a full-moon night.
Wherever I may roam I may create a new home:
But this sense of place has gone.
This was our Mallacoota magic.

Milena Cifali

The wind breathes

The wind breathes.
The curtain trembles.

Bushfires have killed 200 people
all around me
but our house is as yet untouched.

I sit here in the eye
of the oasis of calm
and write this
knowing
somewhere close by
homes are disintegrating
and courageous volunteers
inhale black ash.

There's a thin veil between here and there.

Soon, I could be awoken from deep sleep
by black smoke against white moon
and scorching midnight dawn.
Is there someone on the other side
of this veil…

imagining themselves
sitting on a bed

writing poetry
and safe
instead of caught
like me

in nightmare smoke?

The wind breathes.
The curtain trembles.

Joe Dolce, Cobargo

Honey

Greta's hives burned this summer.
She moved them from fire at Termeil.
Somewhere between Mogo and Broulee,
bees and sweetness perished.

Moya Pacey

Corrugated iron

It was part of our farm, our home,
its dune-like perfection
covered and protected everything.

Whole constructions of curved precision
became part of our landscape;
water tanks, barns, woolsheds,
Murcutt's prize-winning architecture.*

It was 'the white man's bark',*
the percussion of hail
tap-dancing on rooves,
rainfall's serenade.

Until the rains stopped,
the land dried and cracked,
lightning raked down
from waterless clouds,
the no-longer mythic dragons awoke.

Today, crumpled and warped in its grief,
it covers what it could not protect.

Diana Pearce

* *World Archaeology*, Issue 28

Getting used to it

I am getting used to it. I am finding the positives.
I have the VicEmergency app on my phone
that dings when there is a fire
and dings when there is a flood
and dings when a tree falls
and dings to say don't go outside,
you can't breathe the air
the world is not safe

I am getting used to it

when I wake up, the first thing I do is turn on the dings

give us this day our daily dings and forgive us our dings
as we forgive those who have dinged against us

I have absorbed the dings
I am the dings and the dings are me
we are an indivisible being of pure stress
and we will ding forever and ever
amen

endless disaster is an acquired taste
I am getting used to it

when the air is made of smoke
you can sip cheap whisky outside
and it tastes more expensive
so that is nice
I am getting used to it

my friend who hates exercise was going to go for a jog
for her health

but then the air was dangerous so she had to stay inside
for her health
and watch David Attenborough
which was much more fun for her
so that is also nice
she is getting used to it

we shut all the doors and windows to keep the ash out
but then the house got stuffy
so for the first time in my life
I lit a scented candle
and I felt like a very luxurious, elegant princess
so that is also nice
I am getting used to it

my friend lives in Cottlesbridge, right in the fire path
and his father has learned how to use the app
the app from the start of this poem
and he sits in his chair
checking, checking, checking
looking up at his family
looking down and
checking, checking, checking
and he wasn't much good with the iPad before
but now he is getting used to it

I read the news every day
and all the bad dings about sad things fill me with despair
but the police are helping! they are moving journalists
out of bushfire evacuation centres
so that they cannot report on them
so I will no longer have that depressing news to read
so that is also nice

I used to greet new music students by asking
'did you find the place alright?'
which is a hackneyed and unoriginal question
but this week I had two new music students and I asked
'how was breathing on the way here?'
which is a novel and whimsical question
and makes me seem more interesting
so that is also nice

I used to worry about my superannuation
and was I going to have money when I'm old
but I've stopped putting money in super
because I no longer feel the need to consider being old
so that is also nice

it's all very nice
I am looking forward to this century
I am looking forward to the dings
I am looking forward to my life
I am getting used to it

Josh Cake

Roadblocks

Perhaps on New Year's morning
camped on a beach across the Murray from Ulupna
Island, you too saw the mother and her joey
descend an edge gum, mother so far

ahead she seemed — to you as well? — a cruel
educator, drink where the current banked,
cats lapping at a milk saucer,
lope across the campsite, climb a new tree,

climb in wind and gasps to branches
ever thinner and more precarious
until they settled and became the tree.
As a child, did you too drink

from a brook in the Rocky Mountains?
Did your guide tell everyone, *Drink*
enough and your hair will go white, and your soul
will draw pure white light off the glacier?

Perhaps eight hundred kilometres away
your housemate woke champagne-drunk in her swag
to firies evacuating all the forest
humans to Tathra. A townsperson might have taken pity,

made up a corduroy couch thick
with cigarette smoke. Perhaps soul light is
what you see when you're picking lemon myrtle
and the gas mask doesn't quite mask

the haze's nostalgia: campfire in a lover's pores,
her guitar. Army reservists digging pits
to bury 100,000 livestock. Perhaps the chiming
fig leaves will bell like river

against that joey's tongue. A decade ago
on the hottest ever day in Melbourne
you too might have swum in the Yarra with clear skies
to your right, bitumen to your left.

Be honest: did you gun out to the roadblocks,
drink beers in a hot tub in Cottles Bridge
while a few ridges over ash clouds
were hammers and the ground an anvil

and glowing between them an unreality
oranged and whitened in its forge?
Before the dead had been counted
perhaps you too found it wondrous.

Anders Villani

The mountain

The mountain has gone to a fine blue powder
such as I have seen
        in the billowing aura
                around kerosene flame
sprayed from the mouth of a young fire eater.
In a record year
        for the kind of heat
                that melts the bitumen
and bends the frames of powerlines,
a shard of bottle
        in dry growth becomes
                a magnifying glass
for the sun to use, spot-welding leaves
which fuel the volatile
        oils in timber, the wind a fan-
                convection oven
left on for days, its timer switch broken.
The mountain has gone
        to a sifting of grains
                such as I have heard
were all that remained after fires came
and went with the speed
        of quarter horses
                upwind of a cry for help.
No evacuation plan or decision to remain
can change the lie
        of the land or the way
                flame bolts through it
with radiant heat released as spikes of gas
through the burners
        of knot-holes in trees.

    Lightning strike,
arson, climate in a time of denial and change.
The shapes of animals
   on road signs
     in silhouette, now
blackened on the verge.
The mountain has gone.

Anthony Lawrence

Wollemi National Park

Black branches
      form melted ribbons, thin
frond-like leaves
are burnt-out filaments,
              embers whirling like fireflies.
Smoke plumes the hillsides
verticals of rusted red and black
              the graph of loss.

Two hundred million years of survival
              in the balance. Seeding
into narrow ravines, Wollemi pines
      outlived the dinosaurs lumbering
           towards extinction. Now firestorms
bring lightning strikes, new blazes,
mushroom-clouds that overhang horizons
                like despair.

Two juvenile trees, in Sydney's
        Botanic Gardens, stand sentinel
protected by a metal cage, cloned offspring
available at nurseries and on e-bay.
              For $60 a 40cm plant,
$100 for 60cm, you can create
         your own Jurassic backyard.

Tonight the city's
alight with fireworks, burns out
          all knowledge and regret.
Ice tinkles in celebratory glasses.
    Amnesia deforests the past, the light fall
of leaves. Soon you will forget
                there were parklands.

Margaret Bradstock

* December, 2019

Saving the pines

your closest relatives are Hoop and Bunya,
Norfolk, Kauri and Monkey Puzzle.
more of a puzzle how you survived,
weathered the rifting of continents,
the passing of the age of reptiles.
male and female together
in the one tree, dangling male cones
drifting pollen to female cones above,
spiked sputniks of seed unpalatable
to marauding mouths

one of the best-kept secrets in the world,
pathogen-shy Wollemi can be felled
by microscopic life on human boots.
every one of your adult and juvenile trees
shares the exact same DNA.
it was a mega-fire that almost did you in,
the Gospers Mountain wall of flames,
a new phase of what some are calling
the sixth great extinction. all around you
the browned-off silent forest
a more ordinary devastation –
no redemption there

air-dropped in, yellow-jacketed saviours
doused you in water, cascading
fire-retardant on woodland ahead
of the flames. huddled in gorges
against Triassic sandstone cliffs,
you were 'forest-bathing' with a difference.
two on your flank were scorched and scarified

but you survived, as you have snowstorms
and lightning strikes and the towering jaws of sauropods
you roamed the world, once, giant conifers
of Laurasia and Gondwana, then disappeared
shrank back to this precious motherlode,
fires extinguished for now in a daring
human intervention, protected by the seed
of mammals that on warm wet tropical nights
once scurried at your feet

Louise Wakeling

* January 2020

What would my knitting Nanna do?

In need of consolation in a summer that
won't relinquish its lease, I recite the sonnets
you taught me as you knitted couplets

and stitched together metaphysical yarn.
I ration Shakespeare onto my wilted garden –
words drip then evaporate before they hit dirt.

The wind with its smoky, ashen freight arrives
like a grievance not foregone. It's been months since
I could breathe or my eyes could see with clarity.

Disconsolate, I turn on the news.
Denialism of nature's changing course
creeps on its daily petty pace.

Kate Lumley

Heat stroke

The forensics have packed away their instruments,
Dead mulch removed with gloved fingers –
Weeds flattened, spindles of dry grass –

How did it last as long as it did?
How did they?

Pink-bronze metallic like popular jewellery
Azalea flowers are the silent
Sirens of the garden; by midday
They're strung on chokers of ultraviolet.

Pray, another victim, the lovely croton
Its top leaves scorched to polished jet
Tiny leather shoe uppers, while others
Caught at the tips, are two-toned, black-toed/green.

Suburban gardens wait like crêpe
Mourning-wear, still, listless, for the wash.

Barbara Petrie

My Daddy, my hero

Mummy said you won't be home today
You had important work to do that's taken you away
You had to help somebody out so their children could play
And so I guess I won't see you today

Mummy said you went off in your truck
To help another family who was running out of luck
To try and help protect them so in danger they weren't stuck
With your super friends inside your special truck

Mummy said that you were really brave
You were first to take the call when there were people to save
You tried to save their houses and your best is what you gave
And everyone agrees that you were brave

A man gave me something for you today
He said it was a medal for the things you did that day
And he said you were a hero in each and every way
And that is what so many said today

Mummy said the angels made you fly
And took you back home with them somewhere in the sky
To watch me from a special place and help me to get by
Like you did here before you had to fly

David L. Flaxman

Charlotte, the daughter of Andrew O'Dwyer, a volunteer firefighter who was killed in the line of duty, would not leave her father's coffin during his funeral (7 January 2020). She wore her father's firefighting helmet and medal throughout the ceremony.

I tried to sweep the ash away

I tried to sweep the ash away
And as I did I thought today
These ashes are part of someone that
Has lost their home, or habitat.
Or loved ones who could not escape
Or firies, those brave men they say
Who lost their lives trying hard
To save the Wollondilly yard.
And wildlife who have lost their home
With many left, so all alone
Trying to find a leaf or two
To sustain their newborn babies who
Have known just what it is like
To live in bush that's set alight
Where there's nowhere to escape
They tried so hard but we're too late.
And so I stopped and thought a while
And said a prayer as I stood and cried
For those with no place to go home to
Or will have to make their home anew
I observed quite sadly on that ash
And bless those firies who make that dash
To save homes, pets and people where
No one else would ever dare.
So when you sweep the ash that roamed
Remember it was someone's home.

Cate Beresford

No music

Let there be no music,
for there is no music
on the beach at Mallacoota.

Again and again
all is turned to nothing,
the cherished gift, the favourite chair,
the morning bowl and spoon,
photographs and letters.

There is no music in a coffin.
There is none in tree hollows
nor in forks of branches,
no rustle or cry of koalas,
and no birds to make song.

No cattle are lowing,
or sheep bleating
There is no music
on the banks of well-loved rivers,
none in blue sunlight or orange moon.

Hell, inferno, apocalypse,
all clichés crumple and burn
like leaves and photographs.

Let there be no music,
only respectful silence.

John Lowe

Part Four

HOPE

'The melancholy, the hope, proliferation
of freshly green foliage sprouting
      on scarred charcoal trunks.'
              David Atkinson

'a birthing place
for new growth
and undreamt generations.'
Adèle Ogiér Jones

' — a blessing for tomorrow's children
as wind ripples the sand like waves.'
              Laura Jan Shore

Full mast

Yesterday my husband was a firefighter standing tall
while hosing down unforgiving sparks of indignation

Today I am a widow dousing empty days with water
gushing from sorrowful eyes stinging with polluted air

Tomorrow our son will stand with thousands on the frontline
rallying for climate change because his head became hot as his heart
    turned cold

Why can tomorrow not be yesterday's catalyst for action
so today we can fly our flag at full mast?

Kelly Van Nelson

The fire has gone

Our home
Stands stark
Surrounded by a black landscape
The smell of putrid smoke
Mallee stumps glow red

Our home
Cracked windows, burnt eaves
Roof gutters lay twisted on the ground
Water tanks melted

Collapsed sheds
Molten remains of a motorbike
Galah cage, empty, he died
A dead kangaroo
Silence

I hug my family
My tears won't come
Traumatised Border Collie won't leave our side

Days pass
Rains fall
Streams of black ash
Trickle through an alien landscape
Yukkas sprout green
A native lily

The bush grows green again
A few kangaroos return
But the birds have gone
My heart's song, has gone

Jenny Ash

Holding on

Every person sculpts a dream in their hands,
Holding it close to their hearts,
As a cocoon embraces a growing butterfly,
Ensconced in gossamer threads.
In flight, there is delicate grace,
Beauty, even in pain.

The bibliophile hugs books to their chest,
Skies cling fast to the stars.
She sprints through the brush,
Koala bundled snugly in her arms,
Human and animal lives, intertwined,
Carried away from danger,
Towards life.

So, too, we can
Heal, and bring hope
To scarred earth,
Caring for
Our shared home,
Breathing life back into the dream
For peace.

Kathryn Sadakierski

The science of kindness

It's one minute before the scheduled departure time and she is running up the stairs and up the stairs, across the bridge and down, and as her left foot hits the platform the train is there. Someone helps her on board, someone moves up to make room, the doors close. She'll be home within a few hours, weather permitting, and no clear idea of what is waiting for her there. The train rolls through the suburbs and out into the wilds. The cat in her bag is working its way free and the sun is going down, a silhouette against the flames, and the moon is coming up, red on red. Her phone turns itself off and she places it gently in her pocket, leans back in her seat, closes her eyes. When she wakes again, the cat will be curled beside her, purring.

Jen Webb

The green is gone

Undulating browns and blackened spears
stretch down to the sea and ash-ribboned sand.
Here was the green that fed my soul;
verdant shapes and shades, deep shadows
and shafts of cathedral light
played by palms and ferns and trailing vines
amidst soaring gums, all reaching for the sun
to feed their green.

Coastal rainforest now a memory.
This is where I came home,
home for so many.
No rain to sustain the fine balance here
and a lightning strike to end it all.
I am salt-licked from a swim, cleansed
but hollowed out like the fire-ravaged trees
and all I see before me.

I know the bush will regenerate,
already brown-tipped fans of green emerge,
cabbage palms and burrawangs from blackened ground.
Red-tipped leaf-clusters bloom along hardwood trunks
but rainforest without a canopy cannot exist.
I will return after rain predicted for later this week
to witness the spread of green
but can the rainforest return?

Dorothy Swoope

Scorched soul

Dragon's breath, blood-red orange,
Hades' gates, life expunged
Scorching, searing, voracious beast,
endless carnage, remorseless feast
Roaring freight-train without tracks
devouring all and rounding back
Homes ablaze, townships lost,
victims of hell's holocaust

Flora, fauna, sacred place,
no sanctuary, no escape
Sense the fear; hear the cries,
broken, shattered, defenceless lives
Gone the green, shimmer red,
cream and orange, tan bark shed
The blue gum haze of mountain-view,
now Mohawk stands of charcoal blue

Lifeless, silent, no birdsong,
barren, tragic, void, forlorn
Melted, twisted, crumbled ghosts
fed the ever-growing host
Withered, sterile, powdered fate,
once a welcome garden gate
Before was love, now soulless loss.
Each is left to bear the cost

Drought's bone fingers across our land,
yet water sold and rivers drained
No record heat significance,
t'was minimised with arrogance

Fuel reduction deprecated,
lock up the bush overstated
Compounding factors all to blame,
egos now should bow in shame

Horrors witnessed, etched, ingrained,
desperate need of life regain
To normalise, make sense, to stand,
with help from all across the land
A good has come from battles fought,
united stand and generous thought
Compassion flowed like liquid gold,
it reached out true, to shield, enfold

Our nation mourns the endless toll.
The world, it seems, is on that roll
Open doors and dollars pledged,
to rescue, rebuild, pad the edge
Practical, on the ground,
humanity from all astounds
Now we must pick up what's left,
forge on forth although bereft

Leanne Dyson

fire season

smoke cloaks
this city dawn

a sacrifice
of dreams

afar

that angry
red sun

daubs the river
with its

meaning

first poincianas
have

started
their riot

Terry Wheeler

The bush is still singing

in the aftermath
we no longer check fire apps
or horizons for smoke
forget to pay attention
we flatline

Fire maps have settled to a uniform grey. While we apply salve to burnt paws and sew pouches from old sheets for homeless joeys, birds flash and flaunt, brilliant against a charcoal backdrop. Can't help showing off feathers now fire is no competition. The bush is still singing.

Sandra Renew

'The bush is still singing', Heather Campbell, Chief Executive Officer, Bush Heritage Newsletter, January 2020

Rising from the ashes

The fires still come: early and earlier.
But I remember the Glenbrook fires
that laid siege to our lives in sixty-eight
and were held - they retreated
leaving us an empty world –
and these future memories.

Still warm grey ash underfoot
and black scars on my sleeves
where I brushed against a charred tree;
on this fire-emptied hillside,
no birds sing.

Your death was also such a fire
that swept through my mind so many years later.
Some fires cannot be extinguished.
This was one, I had to wait years
for the ashes of my anguish to cool,
and hope the phoenix of our life together
would rise again, in poems perhaps.

As then, slowly waddling across my path
in the post-fire devastation on that hillside,
a small and dusty, unthinking echidna
came from nowhere,
out of the cooling ashes.

Richard Bell

Thirty days after the bushfire

Gushing rain fell on the former fire ground,
fears of frequent reignition finally gone.

Earth still blatantly bleakly charred
with black sticks jaggedly protruding
that were once struggling trees in the dry terrain.

Native animals yet to return,
their once parched but still life yielding habitat
barren of the limited sustenance it once offered.

Spectral tyre tracks in the scorched fields
mark the beginning of the clearing of the destroyed,
the misery of the ruin is countless.

On a scalded black tree trunk
a vivid green shoot defiantly emerges,
insurgence against the annihilation launches.

Acutely felt human emotional wounds
will take much longer to repair.

Rob McKinnon

13

Thirteen seconds of rain fell today
some sieve of conscience
enough to have a spider re set
a filigree of spent gossamer

either side the hours baked away
hardboards caked in a dust of flour
setting on the Mediterranean herbs
no longer happy this far south

we have aged beneath hats
unwashed to bare our tannins
tattoos run to veiny course
wiped clean in the mystery of towels

these delta maps pertaining
swing a mattock if you can
count out the longer shadows
of inky hot and blistered sweat

remember to listen to the drops' blessings
choke down the boot polish of yoke
as you know deep in the strain of things
the time for talking is over

James Walton

Dystopian palette

Monochrome ashscape.
A crevice oozes neon –
Mount Kaputar slugs.

Natalie Cooke

Inspired by an article about the Mount Kaputar slugs that survived the bushfires near Narrabri.

Rebirth

Looking down, through incongruous eyes
Greedy flames from hell, hungrily consume all in its path
Its death-dealing arms spread far and wide,
Cruelly ravishing the Great Land Down Under.

The screams of the beautifully innocent.
Ever a heartbreaking echo in unfortunate ears,
The ears of the bravest of heroes
Battling those red hot unforgiving arms
All carry such sadness, loss, grief
As the once lush land turns to coal

Then, like the spark that set blaze,
The beat of powerful, generous hearts ring true
Throughout the country
Spirits rise and come together
Blowing the smoke-choked sky clear
Cooling the earth with love
Injured creatures embraced by noble healers

Through the redeeming qualities
Of strength, survival, care
We may celebrate tomorrow.

Mickey Martin

Strength

I can still smell that tree,
dry twigs with the scent of tea tree oil
clinging to peeling branches.
They were tough, those trees,
the great Australian dry their heritage,
fire and climate change challenges
which, in true outback spirit they endured.

Theirs the memory of a million years,
a dreamtime presence in their heart to
overcome destruction, survive time,
become symbols of indestructibility.
Their message to humanity is in those ashes.

I watch the embers, see the glow,
hear their song rise in clear air,
know green will emerge victorious.
Their ghostly presence glows survival
their perfume the odour of evermore,
mother earth's precious child.

Their vitality flows into my soul
until I am one with their existence.
I am weak, easily discouraged,
could let tears blind reality, but
I can sing their song,
draw their strength, preserve their message.

Lindsay Coker

a thing to do alone

She walks the scorched embankment,
wants to paint it
    — charcoal against that strange pink.
She needs to see inside there. I watch her
inside there now. Can't see her anymore.

I sit in the car for one great idling second
trying to hear the approaching flame front
    over sluicing traffic,
but I have never heard one.
A freight train, they say.
    You've heard them say that, right?
Like you're tied to the tracks — I suppose.

She's back in the car saying, 'it's eerie,
    you should go in there'
and I'm standing beside hissing traffic.
The burnt air is falling quiet and wet.
My hand against the cool door closing
watching clouds of steam rise from the earth
holding heat
still
all these days after flames peeled the letters
    from our signs.

On a cut stump
fruit skewered on a ring of fencing wire.
You can see it's only the outer layer of bark that's burnt
into the black of damp fur. The circle of oranges
uneaten, but for the swarming ants
those underground creatures, waiting it out

surfacing now, finding a way back from the deep.

I am still waiting
in leaves made golden by heat,
fine veins of white lightning revealing their inscape,
the order in chance
fallen fresh against volcanic ground.

I'm waiting, it's raining and steam is rising.
I'm waiting as she waits,
her mind mixing colours.
And I went in without her
as she without me
as if it is a thing to do alone
like that other thing we have all done
we will all do again.

Gareth Sion Jenkins

Coagulated time

At first it could be any peaceful village clinging
            to the coast, not many shops;
houses with ocean views dot,
        hold fast to the escarpment.

At the heritage wooden wharf, cafe chic
          on the water's edge,
everyone goes about their business.
We scour, investigate beyond the facade
    of appearances, the pretence of resilience.

We search in cul-de-sacs; the burnt-out houses
          and vacant blocks elude us;
    surely they have not been rebuilt.

Walls of flame sear the imagination,
          an ash-filled nightmare,
singed specks float in the scorched air
    and settle bobbing, lapping,
        the troubled sea.

A scalded possum squeals,
    the aftertaste of wildlife.
Gutted houses of the mind
    disappear in an instant.
Sooty time, condensed time coagulated;
        the blood chills in the heat.

Dwellings destroyed at random,
        the occasional one left untouched
in the residual detritus. The placid expression

    of a child's teddy, charred,
            original ears spared.

The melancholy, the hope, proliferation
of freshly green foliage sprouting
        on scarred charcoal trunks.
Houses reappear; the people may be as dust
    but they bear all things,
        endure all things.

David Atkinson

Optimism

Flames devour a sky
ferocious with red
a bitter orange glow
singes air catching on
gum trees   the world ignites –
only a couple of houses lost
and around the village
earth's burnt to cinders
There've been fires before
but not with such intensity.
         Broiling smoke haze
smothers land   sky
and everyone's poised
for another onslaught
if fires flare up again
if winds change direction

On the edge of the Snowies
the village is a green oasis
in a charred landscape
and my friend said
she hadn't heard her
favourite birds for several days
but late yesterday
the distinctive cry
of gang gang cockatoos –
like an old creaky gate –
resounded around the valley
and she smiled
for the first time in ages

Colleen Z. Burke

Aria

The smoke has cleared. Listen –
the birds celebrate dawn.

Who am I to wail
for those I couldn't save;

the bees, koalas, ancient trees.
Surely, I could cough up one note

of hope out of this dry riverbed, herald
the green sprigs rising through ash.

Spit, spit – a curse on cotton farmers, coal
diggers, water stealers.

Calling lost tribes, the ululations in my throat
are visitations by ghosts without names.

When I say, 'I', who might I mean? Not these bones
wrapped in thinning flesh, not this wrinkled face.

I wait for silence to enter me like stones
tossed into a well.

This song is not a rocket ship veering through space.
This song's a dilly bag filled with seeds and grasses.

It's a water hole harbouring new life.

Hush, hush – a blessing for tomorrow's children
as wind ripples the sand like waves.

Laura Jan Shore

The Croajingolong Phoenix

It was 9 am on New Year's Eve
When the deadly firestorm came,
Our dear friend Mallacoota,
Would she ever be the same?

They gathered on the foreshore
When day turned into night,
The fire had surrounded the township,
It was a fearful sight.

Digger said 'I'm not moving,
It's my van I'm going to save!'
You could say he was bloody stupid;
Some would say he was brave.

The destruction it was massive
With the bush and houses destroyed,
The ancient land looked different,
But its spirit had survived,

And in a far-off paddock
On lonely Water Trust Road,
Our three much-loved caravans
Were ready to explode.

Goodbye our dear Lombardi,
The Spaceline and Bernie's Pride,
They faced the fire together,
Standing side by side.

We have seen the heartfelt sadness
Of locals who have lost it all.
How do they move forward,
Will they answer to the call?

But rest assured, our dear friend,
The story, it does not end;
As the phoenix from the ashes rose,
We will return to you again.

Colin Lanphier

Colin's family has been going to Mallacoota for 37 years.
In December 2019, the road closed two days before they were due to leave, and on New Year's Eve their caravan (the Lombardi) was destroyed by fire.

Forest pyre

Like sooty sculptures, they reach for the sky;
A battalion of blackened soldiers,
An eternal reminder of that fiery day,
My forest that was.

The rich habitat it nurtured
Burnt to a charcoal crisp;
It will not regenerate in a few days
What was created over many eons.

Sinkholes of powdery silt
Seemingly sterile and barren:
Ashes to ashes…
Dust to dust.

The blinds have been lifted
As the bloodied sun rises and sets -
No leafy canopy now to veil its glory
As my busy days begin and end.

Hope springs afresh
With signs of new life,
The sculptures erupt with delicate shoots
In gratitude to the rains.

Soft green and pink bouquets
Cling to trunks as black as pitch,
And on the forest floor
The seedbank awaits its moment of glory.

Velvety moss
A patchy carpet
And here and there are wildflowers,
Tiny harbingers of spring.

A paradise lost
But my love is strong;
I am pledged to this land
For all eternity.

Cathy Soulsby

I contemplate my fire

'L'Univers nous reprend,
    rien de nous ne subsiste'

In rapture fall
cruciform inflame
a longing void
proceeding
from the heat
oppressed brain.

Tormented vein of sky
strike in absent light
smouldered soil
distracted shore
this summer day
in night

and on this lake our bodied mass
dark hearts beneath a darkening sky
heavy lungs in breathing in
kind euthanising air
expel the languid rasp
of time
and quivering hands, clinging faith
clawing life-clung pier
this last deceiving chapel;
deaths row where worldly hopes will die a fear

Darkeye and
    ash to ash to ash
    Eternal Circle blind
    and in time
    in ash a flower grew --
    qu'ici-bas tout continue encor

Órlaith Ní Brádaigh

* Epitaph and closing line from 'Triste, Triste'
   (Jules Laforgue)
 'the universe reclaims us/nothing of ours endures'
 'let everything down here continue again'

And if they ask how it happened …

And if they ask how it happened …
We'll talk about the mist,
the benediction of moisture saturating skin,
the cushion of clouds
between us and the valley.

It was the children who believed.

We came to worship the last remnant forest.
Eucalypts with raw, patchy trunks,
tall spines, leaves like tattered wings,
plumes of dun green air. Our nostrils flared.

Below us, derelict buildings.
After the drought, the fires, the floods.
Animal bones mound on street corners.
The persistent stench of death.

We climbed because the children dreamt

of trees. It began as a thought.
They huddled together in a little copse.
Their small faces stern with intent,
backs straight, bare toes pressed into topsoil.

Without a word, hands began to scoop.

They buried each other's feet.
They planted themselves, refusing to move
until roots, like little hairs
pulsed from their soles.

Laura Jan Shore

Mandala, Delicate Nobby Beach

Azure sky, indigo Pacific Ocean receding from the shore, leaving patterns of ash — arcs, curves, where ebbing waves deposit fragments from the fires — brittle leaves of Gum, some just kissed by flames (reds, russets), others umber, charcoal.

A heart-shaped mandala with black volcanic pebbles polished by the sand, pearly cuttlebones of Cuttlefish, shells (big and small), and burnt leaves at the centre. This a sister and I are building for the millions claimed by the flames.

At first we're silent as we place each item combed from the beach. Then in low voices, through half-formed sobs, we share our awareness gleaned from news reports and what we've witnessed.

Homes lost. Food sources gone. Vast tracts of blackened trees and ground. Burn victims screaming, shrieking, howling in excruciating pain.

Then we talk of the deniers arguing against the fires — they refute the climate crisis, blame 'Inner City Greenies', say we should be thinking of the victims.

Around our mandala, white seabird feathers are sentinels quivering on the wind.

Helen Moore

* 27.11.19

Note: Helen Moore deliberately utilises initial capitals to elevate the status of animals and natural phenomena.

Embers

Concise its definition
     : small piece of live coal or wood
     in dying fire
thinking of nightmare coal wrecks
on land gasping for air
in lingering embers,
     : almost extinct residue of activity.
Never extinguished
generations bound to land
wildlife in valleys with ferns
stretching eucalypts
whose ancestors grew
tall ever before
discoveries and businesses
mined earth's coal,
once plant life
too far back to remember.

Still, dreading embers
fanned in wind without age
we dream of fresh life
where smouldering
will produce once again
a birthing place
for new growth
and undreamt generations.

Adèle Ogiér Jones

Rain and Song

1.

When your god is nature
And she is on fire
You can only pray for her tears
Of rain.

2.

How do I pray?
I pray with the tree that has lost its flower
But knows that the spring
Will return

I sit in my car in the rain and I listen
While Joni sings Coyote for the second time
While my seedling carrots drink in the wet
Rain and song, rain and song

3.

There are places
Where you walk the earth
And something calls to you
And you pay attention

Miriam Hechtman

New days

What are new days
made of?
First blue of sky
after dead months
of smoke.
Children setting off
for school
after holidays.
A twisted ankle.
A pebble in the hand
of a man.
Ghosts and auras.
The morning wind
on summer skin.
Coffee, bitter, sweet.
Meeting an old friend
with words of advice,
the two of us
walking the canyons
of the city.
A rush of birds
calling in the trees.
Looking for higher
feelings
inside of me.
Listening, listening
to Lil' Peep
sing 'Liar';
pain in songs,
ain't it strange
that it can make you

feel braver and taller.
I catch a train back
through the Inner West,
watch the sunlight
like a trail of sparks
upon the metal rails.
Out the window
mothers are waving,
cars are caught together
on a narrow road,
and an old guy
with a bag of oranges
walks with a stick,
then stops to rest
in the shade.
New days,
new days,
passing by
hardly noticed
in a pale cool
morning blaze.

Mark Mordue

New hope

The red darkness lifts and daylight shines again
The roar of the fire has passed, the silence is grim
A blackened tree, still burning inside its hollow, crashes to the ground
A cast iron roof sits distorted and buckled amongst the ash
Men sit weary and swore, exhaustion holds them down
They wipe sweat and black ash from their faces
Their time of battle and courage is behind them
Grief floats in, settling over the darkened earth and its people
The loss, raw and real, an ache reaching deep into everyone
And with the daylight, a gathering of support takes true form
The spirit among the people,
driven by compassion touches the lives of many
Hope grows with simple deeds and new friends
A new evening gathers a new faith for all

Vacen Taylor

Emblazoned

The trees were just silhouettes,
Inked etchings, there against
Wavering orange glass,
Like Greek attic vases,
Shadows and cracks in the clay,
Crumbling earth in the blaze.

Sparks of gold curl into the sky,
Replacing the clouds
We used to look up at as kids,
Finding shapes, stories, up in the heavens.

But now, on the singed ground,
A lone horse runs,
A shooting spark,
The phoenix's tail shimmering
As it flies from the ashes,
Seeking shelter from the firestorm.

It is all we can do
To find the truth, to follow trails of light
Out of the dark.

Kathryn Sadakierski

wildflowers bloom in what's left of hope
　　　　　　　　　　　　Ron C. Moss

Acknowledgments

We gratefully acknowledge the following publications in which poems in this anthology first appeared.

Part One

'Black feathers' by Rosa O'Kane was first published in *Not Very Quiet* (Issue 6), 30 March 2020.

'Pyromaniac's Lament' by Peter Mitchell was first published in *Australian Poetry Anthology*, Vol. 7 (eds Yvette Holt and Magan Magan), Melbourne, 2019.

Part Two

'This is not a drill' by Anne Casey was first published in *The Irish Times* (Weekend Review), 11 January 2020.

'Fire' by Gayelene Carbis was first published in *Anecdotal Evidence*, Five Islands Press, Melbourne, 2017.

'I love a sunburnt country' by Niel Smith was first released on YouTube, 11 Jan. 2020 https://youtu.be/uioNNwAftWo

'A new normal' by Mark Roberts was first published in *Bluepepper*, 24 Dec. 2019

'Bushfire Moon (excerpts)' by Ron C. Moss is a selection reinspired by the recent fires, initially contained in his

book of haiku and tanka, also called *Bushfire Moon*, Walleah Press, North Hobart, 2017.

Part Three

'Post inferno' by Tony Steven Williams is a modified version of a poem first published in *MacQueen's Quinterly* (Issue 1), 1 Jan. 2020.

'Firelife' by Gail Willems was first published in *Blood Ties and Crack-Fed Dreams*, Ginninderra Press, Port Adelaide, 2013.

Part Four

'Rising from the ashes' by Richard Bell is a modified version of a poem first published in *Mountain Secrets* (ed. Joan Fenny), Ginninderra Press, Port Adelaide, 2019.

'Forest Pyre' by Cathy Soulsby is based on a poem, 'The Forest' that was self-published in *Burning Love: Fire in my Heart*, Clonbinane, 2010. Cathy was inspired to revisit her original poem in response to the 2019–2020 fires.

'Rain and song' by Miriam Hechtman was first published under the Instagram handle **@_fourlines_**

wildflowers bloom in what's left of hope is a line from the sequence 'Cracked sky' by Ron C. Moss which originally appeared in *Presence Haiku Journal Issue 62*

Biographies

Adèle Ogiér Jones has four collections of poetry, including *Counting the Chiperoni* (Ginninderra Press, 2019). She appears in Ginninderra anthologies *Wild* (2018) and *Mountain Secrets* (2019). Her international works include novel *Desert Diya* (Ginninderra Press, 2010) and *Kabul Football* (www.un.org/disarmament/poetryforpeace/poems).

Alexandra Wallis is fourteen years old and attends Kew High School. During school holidays she stays with her grandparents in Mallacoota. On 31 December 2019, she watched the fire surround, but miss, her grandparents' property. She reluctantly left Mallacoota aboard HMAS *Choules* with her younger brother Nicholas.

Amanda Stewart lives in Forster NSW, surrounded by rich and varied habitats, where she loves to walk and photograph the birds. She wrote 'Seven snapshots of the east coast fires' in November 2019, while watching the fires rage through the coastal forests.

Anders Villani is the author of *Aril Wire* (Five Islands Press, 2018). He holds an MFA from the University of Michigan's Helen Zell Writers' Program, where he received the Delbanco Prize for poetry. He was born and lives in Melbourne.

Angela Costi is the author of four poetry collections, include *Honey and Salt* (Five Islands Press, 2007) and *Lost in Mid-Verse* (Owl Publishing, 2014). Receiving a travel award from the National Languages Board, she studied Ancient Greek drama in Greece (1995), and also worked in Japan on a collaboration involving her poetry, funded by the Australia Council (2009).

Anne Casey is a former environment journalist/author, with work widely published internationally, ranking in *The Irish Times*' Most Read. Author of two poetry collections, *where the lost things go* and *out of emptied cups*, she has won/been shortlisted for awards in Ireland, Northern Ireland, the UK, the USA, Canada, Hong Kong and Australia.

Anthony Lawrence has published fifteen books of poetry and a novel. His most recent collection, *Headwaters* (Pitt Street Poetry, 2016) won the 2017 Prime Ministers Literary Awards (Poetry). He teaches Creative Writing at Griffith university and lives on Moreton Bay, Queensland.

Ash Spring is a freelance editor and a self-published author of predominantly LGBT+ science-fiction/fantasy novels, who also dabbles in writing poetry, short fiction, and lyrics. Living in Perth, Western Australia, Ash graduated from Murdoch University with a degree in English and Creative Writing.

Audrey Molloy is an Irish poet based in Sydney, with work published in *The North, Magma, Mslexia, The Moth, The Irish Times, Meanjin, Cordite, Overland, Verity La* and *Australian Poetry Journal*. In 2019 she received a number of prestigious awards. Her debut pamphlet, *Satyress*, was published by Southword Editions (2020). www.audreymolloy.com

Ava Mendoza is a Year 6 student who lives on the beautiful Mornington Peninsula in Victoria. She enjoys writing short stories that keep readers on edge, and then hits them with a dramatic ending. In her spare time, she enjoys playing netball, reading, drawing and spending time with her spoodle, Hazel.

Barbara Petrie, novelist, dramatist and poet, is the author of *Farrow Night* (Island Press); *Kiwi & Emu, an Anthology of Contemporary Poetry by Australian & New Zealand Women*, and *William Hart-Smith: Hand to Hand: A Garnering*, Ed, (Butterfly Books); and several collections of Blue Mountains poetry (Ed). Most recent work is an historical novel set in pre-European New Zealand.

Beatriz Copello (Dr) writes poetry, fiction, reviews and plays. Her poetry books include *Women Souls and Shadows, Meditations at the Edge of a Dream, Flowering Roots, Under the Gums Long Shade,* and *Lo Irrevocable del Halcon* (Spanish). She has been published in *Southerly*, *Australian Women's Book Review* and in feminist publications.

Brenda Proudfoot is a teacher and writer who lives in the Hunter Valley. Raised in New Zealand, she has a keen interest in Australian flora and fauna. Her short stories and creative non-fiction have been published by Catchfire Press, Spineless Wonders, the Hunter Writers Centre and *The Newcastle Herald*.

Brenda Saunders is a Wiradjuri writer from Sydney. Author of three poetry collections, her work appears in *Australian Poetry Journal*, *Overland, Southerly and Westerly*. Winner of the Oodgeroo Noonuccal Prize (Queensland Poetry) and the Joanne Burns Award for Prose Poetry (*Spineless Wonders*) in 2018, Brenda is a mentor for *Black Cockatoo* at https://verityla.com/

Carolyn Gerrish is a Sydney poet who has published five collections of poetry, the latest being *The View from the Moon* (Island Press, 2011). She enjoys performing her work and is currently working on her sixth collection.

Cate Beresford worked as a technical writer before penning articles for magazines and writing her first novel *Seven Signs*. She recently released her first young adult fiction, *Bass Point Boys* and has also published three books of verse. Cate is an active member of the Shellharbour Writers group.

Cathy Soulsby lives surrounded by nature in the Great Dividing Range, near Broadford, Victoria. She began writing poetry after the Black Saturday wildfires of 2009, and it proved to be great therapy. These days, she writes on anything which inspires her. She is currently writing about COVID-19, and finishing her memoirs.

Cheryl Pearson lives in Manchester, United Kingdom. Her poems have been published in *The Guardian, The Moth, Qu* and *Mslexia*, and she has twice been nominated for a Pushcart Prize. Her first full poetry collection, *Oysterlight*, was published in 2017 (Pindrop Press), and *Menagerie* in 2020 (The Emma Press).

Chris Considine lives in Plymouth, United Kingdom. She has published five poetry collections with Peterloo Poets and Cinnamon Press. Her most recent publication is *Seeing Eye* (Cinnamon Press, 2019). Her son is a member of the Fire Services in Australia.

Colin Lanphier and his family have holidayed in Mallacoota's caravan park for the last thirty-seven years; it is their second home. In December 2019, the road closed two days before they were due to leave, and on New Year's Eve their caravan (the Lombardi) was destroyed by fire.

Colleen Z. Burke's most recent and twelfth poetry collection is *Sculpting a Landscape* (2019). She has also published two memoirs: *The Waves Turn* (2016) and *The Human Heart is a Bold Traveller* (2017) and is co-editor of the anthology *The Turning Wave: Poems and Songs of Irish Australia*.

Daragh Byrne is Irish born, now living, working and writing in Sydney, Australia. With a background in physics, a professional life of building software, and a longstanding study (and teaching) of meditation, he writes to explore the dichotomies of existence and the eternal balancing act between joy and sorrows.

Darrell Coggins is a poet, visual artist and musician. He has poems published in a number of literary journals including *Poetry Matters, Positive Words, Tamba, Studio* and *Friendly Street Poetry Anthologies*.

Dave Kavanagh is husband to Ber, proud father of Adam and Rou, Managing Editor of Irish literary journal *The Blue Nib*, organic gardener, part-time island recluse. He is often found skulking behind a computer or with his head buried in a book. His first novel, *The Tangle Box*, is scheduled for release (Adelaide Books, 2021).

David Atkinson is a Sydney-based poet who has been published widely in Australia and the USA and in the UK. His favoured areas for poetic expression include the human condition and the natural world. His collection *The Ablation of Time* is published by Ginninderra Press (2018).

David L. Flaxman is a resident of the Hawkesbury area in NSW. A family man, he is a proud parent to five wonderful children who provide never-ending sources of inspiration and enjoyment. He also takes a keen interest in sports, writing and community.

Diana Pearce has an M.A. in writing from UTS, where her poetry supervisor was the late Martin Harrison. The "everyday" inspires her poetry; urban development, childhood memories, domestic activities and her environment. Her poems have been published in a variety of outlets, many in *The Mozzie*, her work has also received awards in regional competitions

Dorothy Simmons is an Irish-Australian writer living in Albury, New South Wales. A retired teacher, her life has always revolved around words and ideas and their capacity to change lives. Her three Rs are reading, 'riting and running. Samples of her work can be found at www.dorothysimmons.org

Dorothy Swoope is an award-winning poet, published in print and online in newspapers, anthologies and literary magazines in Australia, the USA and Canada. Her memoir, *Wait 'til Your Father Gets Home!* was released in 2016. She lives on the South Coast of New South Wales, Australia.

Ellen Shelley is a Newcastle poet. She reads at local poetry events and has been published widely, including in *Eureka*, *Backstory*, *Other Terrain*, *Not Very Quiet*, *Eucalypt*, *The Blue Nib* and *The Canberra Times*. She was Highly Commended in the Philip Bacon Ekphrasis Award.

Emma Briggs is an environmental activist and poet, recently publishing *For Life*, a book of poems largely themed around climate change. She regularly writes poetry, articles and stories on the 'Medium' platform. She returned to dry land five years ago, having previously sailed the world on Greenpeace ships for fifteen years. http://www.emmabriggs.net/

Erin Frances is currently studying English and French at the University of Sydney. Her poetry has been published in *The Blue Nib*. In her spare time, she enjoys swimming, figure skating, reading with cats, and walking her toy poodle.

Fotoula Reynolds is a retired Education Support Worker. She lives in the Dandenong Ranges in Victoria where she manages and co-ordinates an open-mic poetry event in her local community. She has published three poetry collections. Her work appears locally and internationally and she is also a Pushcart Prize nominee.

Gail Willems is a retired nurse currently living in Mandurah, Western Australia. Her poetry has been published in Australia, United Kingdom, New York, Lisbon, Belgium, New Zealand, in journals, magazines, anthologies, and 5UV Writers Radio. Gail's first poetry collection, *Blood Ties and Crack Fed Dreams* was published 2013 by Ginninderra Press

Gareth Sion Jenkins is the editor of *The Toy of the Spirit* (Puncher & Wattmann, 2019), the first book-length publication of writings by Anthony Mannix. His poetry collection *Recipes for the Disaster* was published by Five Islands Press (2019). He archives and publishes at [Apothecary Archive http://apothecaryarchive.com/](http://apothecaryarchive.com/)

Gary Colombo De Piazzi finds joy playing with words, mixing and shuffling them to catch a moment, trace an emotion, shift a perception. Conveying simplicity with perceptivity in haiku is his holy grail.

Gayelene Carbis is an award-winning writer of poetry, prose and plays. Her first book of poetry, *Anecdotal Evidence* (Five Islands Press, 2017) was awarded Finalist in the International Book Awards (2019). Her work has been widely published and performed in Australia and overseas. She teaches Creative Writing at Sandybeach and English/EAL at ACU.

Geoff Callard is a New Zealander living in Melbourne. He has been a feature poet at *Be Mused Poetry* and at the Australian launch for the anthology *Planet in Peril*, and has published work in the *Golden Walkman* magazine, *Planet in Peril* (Fly on the Wall Press, 2019) and *Write to the River*.

Geoffrey Bonwick is a trauma informed therapist. He has interviewed and treated, pro bono, over a dozen people who had direct experience of the fires either in Eastern Victoria or Southern NSW.

George Clark lives on a farm in the central tablelands. He writes when anguish or grace or beauty comes upon him. He believes in narrative, nature and the natural order of things. He finds meditation and silence is a form of prayer, particularly after a glass of his own wine.

Hazel Hall is a widely published Canberra poet and musicologist. Her recent collections include *Step by Step: Tai Chi Meditations* with Angie Egan (Picaro Poets, 2018), *Moonlight over the Siding* (Interactive Press, 2019), and *Severed Web,* a collection of climate change haiku with artist Deborah Faeyrglenn (Picaro Poets, 2020).

Helen Budge is a poet whose work has been read on the ABC and featured as part of the *Trove Project (UWA): Digital Display*. Her poems appear in publications, such as *Tamba, The Mozzie, Valley Micropress (NZ), Yellow Moon, Fremantle Arts Review, Westerly, Poetry d'Amour, Creatrix 2012–2016* and *Australian Love Poems 2013*.

Helen Moore is an internationally acclaimed British ecopoet with three published poetry collections: *Hedge Fund, And Other Living Margins* (Shearsman Books, 2012); *ECOZOA* (Permanent Publications, 2015); & *The Mother Country* (Awen Publications 2019), exploring British colonial history in Scotland and Australia and themes of dispossession. www.helenmoorepoet.com

Irina Frolova is a Russian-born Australian poet who lives on the Awabakal land. Her work has appeared in *Not Very Quiet, Australian Poetry Collaboration, Baby Teeth Journal* and *The Blue Nib*. She is currently working on a bilingual pocketbook of poems (Flying Island Books/ASM/Cerberus Press, 2020).

Ivy Ireland is the author of poetry collections *Incidental Complications* (Poets Union, 2007) and *Porch Light* (Puncher & Wattmann, 2015). Her literary awards include the Australian Young Poet Fellowship, the Harri Jones Memorial Prize and the Thunderbolt Prize. She completed her PhD in 2013 and her poetry, essays and reviews have been widely published in journals and anthologies.

Jai Thoolen is a forty-something Mornington Peninsula man who writes children's books, poetry and lyrics. He has a love of rhyme and is not afraid to use it, often. Jai likes to perform at schools and at functions. Lawson is his favourite poet and Pratchett his favourite author. You can find his poetry and other work at www.picklepoetry.com

James Walton was a librarian, a farm labourer, and mostly a public sector union official. He is published in many anthologies, journals and newspapers. His poetry collections include *The Leviathan's Apprentice* (Strzelecki's Lover Press, 2015, *Walking Through Fences* (Flying Island Books, 2018), *Unstill Mosaics* (2019) and *Abandoned Soliloquies* (UnCollected Press, 2019).

Jane Baker lives and writes in the Southern Tablelands of NSW and has experienced, personally, five major bushfires in her lifetime. She is a wildlife carer, a poet, a former high school teacher and a columnist.

Jane Downing has poetry published around Australia including in *Eureka Street, Poetrix, Cordite, Rabbit, The Canberra Times*, and *Best Australian Poems* (2004 and 2015). Her collection *When Figs Fly* was published by Close-Up Books (2019).
www.janedowning.wordpress.com

Jeltje Fanoy has been involved with poetry small presses in Melbourne since the seventies and is a founding member of Collective Effort Press and the Melbourne Poets Union. She calls herself a 'minimalist traveller', crafting everyday spoken language into collage-like pieces marked by an apparent simplicity and emphatic directness.

Jen Webb is Distinguished Professor of Creative Practice, and Dean of Graduate Research, at the University of Canberra. She has published eighteen poetry collections and artist books, and is co-editor of the Mandarin/English anthology *Open Windows: Contemporary Australian Poetry*. Her most recent book is *Moving Targets* (Recent Work Press, 2018).

Jenny Ash was born and lived in Port Lincoln until moving to Woodcroft in 2016. The Port Lincoln area has experienced devastating bushfires in which tragically people died and homes were lost. The aftermath of the bushfires was traumatic, and she realised that life would never be the same again. She tried to capture her emotions in her poetry.

Joe Dolce is a much-awarded composer and poet, and recipient of the University of Canberra Health Poetry Prize (2017) and the 25th Launceston Poetry Cup. His work is published widely, including in *Meanjin*, *Southerly*, *Canberra Times*, *Quadrant*, *North of Oxford* (US) and *Antipodes* (US). His collection *On Murray's Run: Poems and Lyrics* was published by Ginninderra Press (2017).

John Lowe, a retired librarian, assesses poetry for Virginia's Create a Kids' Book service. He has published verse in *Blast, Poetry Monash, Off the Path, Once upon a Sonnet, Poetry d'Amour* and Deakin Literary Society anthologies, and articles on Lawrence's *Kangaroo*. With his wife Virginia, he has co-published *Lines Between (Chapbook #27,* Melbourne Poets Union, 2019*)*.

Josh Cake is a writer and performer from Melbourne. He has worked in Italy, France, and Australia. His recent work includes a TEDx talk, a season of online comedy videos, and a heap of live comedy, poetry, and music. www.joshcake.com

Juleigh Howard-Hobson is a poet whose work has appeared in a wide variety of publications, including *Think Journal* and *Great Weather for Media*. She is a Million Writers 'Notable Writer'. Her prizes include the ANZAC Day Award (1980) and the Aelfred (2014), as well as several nominations. Her fifth and most recent book is *Our Otherworld* (Red Salon Press, 2018).

Julian O'Dea is a retired government scientist who is based in Canberra. He began writing poetry a few years ago. His work has appeared in *Creatrix*, *Ygdrasil*, *Friday's Poems*, *The Blue Nib* and other publications.

Julie Annette King was born and grew up in Perth and now resides in Wanneroo. She has engaged in creative writing from a young age. Now semi-retired, she is focusing on blogging, poetry and participating in groups of like-minded people.

Kate Lumley is a Sydney-based writer who has been published in *Studio*, *The Mozzie*, anthologies *Australian Love Poems* (Inkerman & Blunt, 2013), *Prayers of a Secular World* (Inkerman & Blunt, 2015), *To End All Wars* (Puncher and Wattmann, 2018), and *41 Arguments Avant La Lettre* (2020). She was highly commended in the Adrien Abbot poetry prize (2014).

Kathleen Panettieri lives in Chelsea, Victoria and has been writing poetry for over thirty years. Her collection *Trails of Light* was published in 2018, and she has had poems placed in competitions, magazines and anthologies. She has her own poetry page on Facebook, also called Trails of Light.

Kathryn Fry has had poems published in various anthologies and journals, including *Antipodes, Cordite Poetry Review, Westerly, Shuffle, Not Very Quiet*, and *Plumwood Mountain Journal*. Her first collection is *Green Point Bearings* (Ginninderra Press, 2018).

Kathryn Sadakierski's writing has appeared in *The Bangor Literary Journal, The Ekphrastic Review, Nine Muses Poetry, Teachers of Vision,* and *Dime Show Review*. She graduated *summa cum laude* from Bay Path University in Longmeadow, Massachusetts with a Bachelor of Arts degree, and is currently pursuing her Master of Science degree.

Kelly Van Nelson is the #1 bestselling author of *Graffiti Lane: A Poetry Collection* (Making Magic Happen Press, 2019). Her work has featured in numerous international publications. She's a KSP First Edition Fellowship recipient, AusMumpreneur 'Big Idea' Award winner for social economic impact, and winner of Roar Success Awards for Best Book and Most Powerful Influencer www.kellyvannelson.com.

Kirily Isherwood is an animal lover and mother to three and works for a disability charity. She dabbles in writing and other artistic pursuits. Living on a mountain in the beautiful Gold Coast hinterland, where it can be fire one day and flood the next, keeps life interesting.

Kit (Christopher) Kelen has published widely since the seventies, and has a dozen full-length collections in English as well as translated books of poetry in Chinese, Portuguese, French, Italian, Spanish, Indonesian, Swedish and Filipino. His latest volume of poetry in English is *Poor Man's Coat: Hardanger Poems* (UWAP, 2018).

KL Morris has resided in Canberra for five years and is studying writing at the University of Canberra. She has been published in the *UC Anthologies, First, Analecta* and the *UC Writers Zine*. She was a member of the ACT Writers Centre's prestigious HARDCOPY writers' development program in 2019.

Lance Convey lives in Brisbane. An expat from California thirty years ago, he now enjoys slaving away at his business and keeping his wallet open for his four daughters and lovely wife. One day he hopes to get abducted by aliens to their planet so he can write poetry full time.

Laura Jan Shore is the author of poetry collections *Breathworks* (Dangerously Poetic Press, 2002), *Water over Stone* (Interactive Press, 2011), winner of IP Picks Best Poetry (2011), and *Afterglow* (Interactive Press, 2020). Her work has appeared on four continents. In 2019, she received her MFA in poetry from Pacific University. She lives on the far North Coast of NSW.

Leanne Dyson lives near Sarsfield, not far from Clifton Creek, two of the most heavily bushfire impacted areas in East Gippsland. Her family has lived in this region since c. 1870. She self-published a coffee-table book titled, *Darkness and Light 1: East Gippsland Pictures and Poems* (2019).

Les Wicks has toured widely both in Australia and overseas and has work published in over 350 magazines, anthologies and newspapers across thirty countries in fifteen languages. His fourteenth book of poetry is *Belief* (Flying Islands, 2019).

Lilian Cohen is a Melbourne-based writer of poetry and fiction, and has lived abroad for many years. Her work has been published in journals and anthologies in Australia, Israel and the USA. In 2017 she was awarded second prize in the Boroondara Short Story Competition and is currently completing a crime novel.

Linda Adair is a poet and publisher of Rochford Press. Her work was published in the anthology *To End All Wars* (Puncher and Wattmann, 2018), and has appeared in various online journals. Her first collection of poetry, *The consequences of the shattering*, has been selected for the 2020 Melbourne Poets Union Chapbook Series.

Linda Menzies lives in Fife, Scotland; her working life was spent in journalism and public relations. Linda is published in *New Writing Dundee*, *East Lothian Life*, *Shortbread*, *The Writers Café*, *Algebra of Owls*, *Domestic Cherry*, *Contour*, and others. She has produced two collections: *Epiphanies* (2009) and *Into the Light* (2014) and a novel, *A Unicorn on The Meadows* (2018).

Lindsay Coker has been written on developments in medicine and science for country people, as well as writing the op-ed monthly column 'down under' for the Emmitsberg News-Journal in Maryland, USA, for over sixteen years. Now retired and living on the Mornington Peninsula, he has time to indulge his passion for words and poetry.

Louise Wakeling is a poet who lives in the Blue Mountains. Her third collection, *Paragliding in a War Zone*, was published by Puncher & Wattmann (2009). Her fourth, *Off Limits*, will be published in 2020. She is currently writing a fictional exploration of family dysfunction in the 1950s–70s.

Margaret Bradstock has eight published collections of poetry, including *The Pomelo Tree* (Ginninderra Press, 2001 and winner of the Wesley Michel Wright Prize), *Barnacle Rock* (Puncher & Wattmann, 2013 and winner of the Woollahra Festival Award) and *Brief Garden* (Puncher & Wattmann, 2019). Editor of *Antipodes* and *Caring for Country*, Margaret won the Banjo Paterson Poetry Award in 2014, 2015 and 2017.

Marilyn Humbert lives in the northern suburbs of Sydney NSW. Her tanka and haiku appear in Australian and international journals, anthologies and online. Her free verse poems have been awarded prizes in competitions.

Mark Mordue is a Sydney-based journalist and poet. His poetry collection *Darlinghurst Funeral Rites* was published in Australia (Transit Lounge, 2018) and republished in the USA (Reprobate Books, 2019) as a 'flip book' along with a selection of his other poetry under the titles *Poems from the South Coast* and *Phone Poems*.

Mark Roberts is a writer, critic and publisher based in the Blue Mountains, west of Sydney. He has been widely published in numerous journals and magazines since the 1980s. Mark is the founding editor of Rochford Street Review (https://rochfordstreetreview.com/), and has been involved in small literary publishing for over thirty years. His latest collection is *Concrete Flamingos* (Island Press, 2016).

Mary Chydiriotis is a social worker and writer living in Melbourne. Her poems have been published in journals and anthologies in Australia and overseas, including *Social Alternatives*, *Right Now: Human Rights in Aust-ralia*, *Offset* and *Tincture*. Mary's first poetry collection is *Loud and Red* (Ginninderra Press, Picaro Poets series, 2020).

Michelle Brock is a Queanbeyan poet, short story writer and member of the *Limestone Tanka Poets*. Her tanka poems, prose and haiga have been published inter-nationally She was selected to co-judge the 2019 Tanka Society of America's competition. Michelle finds inspiration along rivers and beaches and in everyday moments.

Mickey Martin is a lover of Australia's nature and animals, and growing up in the country is aware that Australia is no stranger to the devastation created by bushfires. She is absolutely honoured to be a part of this anthology, in order to help her countrymen and women.

Milena Cifali lost her home in the Mallacoota bushfires on New Year's Eve 2019. A singer/songwriter, Milena has turned adversity into a positive, rising from the ashes with her book 'Mallacoota Time' a bushfire memoir describing her own personal journey towards recovery, with reflections on home and homelessness. https://www.echobooks.com.au/biography/mallacoota-time.

Miriam Hechtman is a Sydney-based writer, poet and creative producer, writing under the Instagram handle @_fourlines. Founder/host of POETICA, an open mic night for poetry and music in Bondi, she has written and performed her poetry for several organisations, including Australia ReMADE for which she is the current Poet Laureate.

Moya Pacey is a Canberra-based poet. Her most recent poetry collection is *Black Tulips* (Recent Work Press, 2017). Her next collection will be published by Recent Work Press in 2020. She co-edits the online journal, *Not Very Quiet* notveryquiet.com.

Nardine Sanderson is a Geelong-born writer and poet whose love of words stretches across the sea, to immortalise those she loves so that they will love forever.

Natalie Cooke is based in Canberra and writes poetry and fiction for children and adults. She was a Katharine Susannah Pritchard Fellow (2019) and was awarded the June Shenfield Poetry Prize (2018). She has a particular interest in the interaction between humans and the Australian landscape.

Natalie D-Napoleon is from Fremantle, Australia. Her writing has appeared in *Southerly, Westerly, Griffith Review*, and *Australian Poetry Journal*. She won the Bruce Dawe National Poetry Prize (2018). Her debut poetry collection is *First Blood* (Ginninderra Press, 2019).

Nick Allen is the author of *The Riding* and the pamphlet *The Necessary Line* (Half Moon Books, 2017). A collaboration, *Between Two Rivers*, was published by Maytree Press (2019). His poetry appears in anthologies *Verse Matters* and *The Valley Press Anthology of Prose Poetry*, and in a range of other publications.

Niel Smith is a Perth-based spoken word artist, father of five and primary school principal. His work often carries a socio-political theme. Niel has performed across Perth venues and represented Western Australia at the Australian Poetry Slam in 2018 and 2019, finishing sixth and fourth respectively.

Órlaith Ní Brádaigh, a twenty-year old poet, gathered with eight close friends on a small boat moored near Mallacoota's shore at the end of 2019. There she witnessed the power of nature which humanity is often all too powerless to control.

Patricia O'Gready has five self-published poetry books and in earlier years was published in University publications. She has experienced the fear of out-of-control bushfires while living in Bundeena in the Royal National Park south of Sydney.

Peter Mitchell resides in Lismore in Bundjalung Country. His writing is published in international and national print and online journals, magazines and anthologies and he is the recipient of awards, fellowships, mentorships and a writer's grant. He has authored poetry chapbooks, *Conspiracy of Skin* (Ginninderra Press, 2018) and *The Scarlet Moment* (Picaro Press, 2009).

Rebecca Trowbridge has been a soldier, a geologist and now juggles family, high school teaching and writing. She has lived and worked around Australia from the outback to the coast. She has a Master of Science in Volcanology and wants you to know that lava flows downhill.

Richard Bell retired from quantitative psychology eight years ago to concentrate on a life of doing as little as possible. Life events intervened. After forty years, he returned to writing poems, and published his collection *Such Sweet Sorrow* (Ginninderra Press, 2019).

Richard Soloway studied law, comparative religions, English literature and computer science. He has worked in mineral exploration, and has owned a property on the Monaro. In the 1980s he returned to education as a teacher and lecturer and has had articles about computing and some poems published.

Rob McKinnon lives in the Adelaide Hills, South Australia. His poetry has previously been published in the *Wellington Street Review*, *Sūdō Journal*, *Sage Cigarettes Magazine*, *Re-Side Magazine*, *Nightingale & Sparrow Literary Magazine*, *Black Bough Poetry*, *Dissident Voice*, *Tuck Magazine* and *InDaily*.

Rob Schackne was born in New York, and lived in many countries until Australia finally took him in. He now lives in a small Victorian country town, and enjoys the fresh air, the birds and the sunshine. Rob listens to the Grateful Dead. When he's not writing, he likes taking photographs.

Robin Purdey was five years old when her family home in Western Victoria was burnt out in Western. Sixty years later, fires in the high country burned only a few short kilometres up the mountain from her home.

Robyn Sykes has been published in journals and anthologies nationally, internationally and online. Her work draws on her fascination with nature, human behaviour and the idiosyncratic. An entertainer and science graduate, she has studied crocodiles, peered down electron microscopes and lived in Japan. Robyn lives on a farm in south-west NSW.

Ron C.. Moss is a volunteer firefighter who has served with the Tasmanian Fire Service for over twenty years, as well as fighting campaign fires in three states of Australia. Ron is also an internationally awarded poet and artist. His haiku collection *The Bone Carver* (Snapshot Press, 2014) gained multiple awards.

Rosa O'Kane is a Canberra-based poet who grew up in Northern Ireland. Her poem 'Hydrography of the heart' was a commended entry in The Hippocrates Prize (2014). Rosa has been twice shortlisted for the ACU poetry prize. Her poems have been published in *The Canberra Times*, *Not Very Quiet* and *The Blue Nib*.

Rosie Jackson lives in Frome, UK. Her poems are widely published and have won many awards. Books include *What the Ground Holds* (Poetry Salzburg, 2014), *The Light Box* (Cultured Llama, 2016); *Two Girls and a Beehive*, poems about Stanley Spencer (Two Rivers Press, 2020). Rosie was in Australia during the worst of the bushfires in 2020. www.rosiejackson.org.uk

Sam Middleton is founder of the 'Celebrating Red Gums' initiative and is passionate about inspiring and facilitating expressions of connectivity with the Australian landscape. Her signature style of poetry reflects a love of entertaining through humorous verse and the showcasing of understated Aussie wit.

Sandra Renew has poetry recently published in *Griffith Review* (Griffith University), *The Blue Nib*, *The Canberra Times*, *Hecate*, *Axon*, and *Australian Poetry Journal (2019)*. Her recent collections are *Acting Like a Girl* (Recent Work Press, 2019) and *The Orlando Files* (Ginninderra Press, 2018).

Simone King is a Melbourne-based writer. She won the Good Grief Award in the Australian Grieve Writing Competition (2018), was highly commended for the June Shenfield Poetry Award (2019), and has been shortlisted for other poetry prizes. Simone's writing is published in a range of journals, magazines and anthologies.

Siobhan Hodge has a PhD in English literature. She won the Kalang Eco-Poetry Award (2017) and Patricia Hackett Award for poetry (2015), and has had poetry and critical work published and translated in a range of places, including *Westerly, Southerly, Overland* and *Cordite*. Her first chapbook is *Justice for Romeo* (Cordite Books, 2018).

Stephen House has won two AWGIE Awards, Rhonda Jancovic Poetry Awards and more, and was shortlisted for Lane Cove Poetry, Overland Fiction, Patrick White Playwright, Queensland Premiers Drama, Tom Collins Poetry, Greenroom acting Awards and more. He received Ozco Canada and Ireland residencies, and an Asialink India Residency. He's published often.

Steve Boyce sees himself as a storyteller in verse, that sometimes rhymes, sometimes beats and often just is what it is. One day he hopes to decide which.

Susan Hawthorne is the author of eight collections of poetry. Her eco-poetry book *Earth's Breath* (Spinifex Press, 2009) was shortlisted for the Judith Wright Poetry Prize (2010). Her other books include *Cow* (Spinifex Press, 2011), shortlisted for the Kenneth Slessor Poetry Prize, *Lupa and Lamb* (Spinifex Press, 2014), and most recently *The Sacking of the Muses* (Spinifex Press, 2019).

Susan Wakefield is a freelance writer, novelist and published poet who recently returned to Australia from twenty years abroad. Susan has worked as an editor, ghostwriter and speech writer, and as a freelance political writer and proofreader for various publications including *The Boston Globe* and *The New York Times*.

Tegan Jane Schetrumpf is a poet and academic. A firm believer in interdisciplinary study, she has a Bachelor of Medical Science, and her Master of Letters in English from the University of Sydney. Her postgraduate research into traditional form and narrative in millennial Australian poetry won the university's Dame Leonie prize (2015).

Terry Wheeler worked in the public service for decades and was inspired to write after seeing Michael Dransfield's poems in *The Australian* when a teenager. Terry has been published in Australia and abroad since retiring. He lives in Brisbane when not travelling.

Toby Davidson is a senior lecturer at Macquarie University, Sydney. His first collection *Beast Language* (Five Islands Press, 2012) has been anthologised in *Contemporary Australian Poetry*, *The Fremantle Press Anthology of Western Australian Poetry*, *The Weekly Poem* and *Best Australian Poems*. His second collection, *Four Oceans*, will be published by Puncher and Wattmann (2020).

Tony DeLorger was born in Sydney but now resides in Adelaide, having written full time since 1999. He is a novelist, author of both fiction and non-fiction, poetry and plays. His work thus far includes twenty-one published works, of which eight are poetry.

Tony Steven Williams is a Canberran poet, short-fiction author and songwriter. His debut poetry collection is *Sun and Moon, Light and Dark* (Ginninderra Press, 2018). Tony and his artist wife Arlene directly experienced the Ash Wednesday fires in Adelaide in 1983 and the bushfires in Canberra in 2003.

Vacen Taylor is a children's author with a portfolio of screenwriting and stage play achievements. A selection of her poetry has been published in art and literature journals. One of her plays was selected to be part of the Playwrights Program 2017 and then directed and performed as a performance reading.

Virginia Lowe (Dr) has poems published in forty paper and digital journals and anthologies, including *Here is Home* (NLA Publishing, 2019), *Journal of Postcolonial Writing* and *Poetry D'Amour 2017*. With her husband John, she co-published *Lines Between (Chapbook #27, Melbourne Poets Union, 2019)*. Her academic work is *Stories, Pictures and Reality: Two Children Tell* (Routledge, 2006). www.createakidsbook.com.au

The House at Rosedale

The picture on the cover of this book represents all that is left of the house Helen Gamble's family called their second home for more than four decades. Helen's story describes the love, laughter and friendship that the house embodied, sentiments echoed by all those families who lost properties.

The block at the end of the point facing the island, always ours, chosen by Mum, Dad and the junior members of our team aged 10 and 12, our caravan put in place at once to reserve the spot. Named 'Rosehill' by Dad to acknowledge the Gamble's house at Rosedale. A good decision, never regretted, as the best place for us on the coast.

A house built by Herman, the Swiss builder, to his design, influenced by Dad's insistence on a butterfly roof, far bigger than the two rooms inside because it covered the outdoor living and carport. The intention was to gather as much rainfall for the tank as possible. No water or electricity on tap in those days. It was tank water, complete with dead rats usually discovered well into our stay, and candles, kerosene fridge and lamps, an Esky for the drinks and a two-ring gas stove to feed four, six, ten or more, depending on the guest list. All this operated by a mechanically-minded Mum, while Dad experimented with a nine-volt electric light system, a self-powered electric shower brought from PNG and, his real love, an underwater diving breathing system, with its motor in the rowing boat and a garden hose to feed the diver.

The design of the house was perfect, for us. The 'outdoor living', facing north to catch the sun in winter but protected from the southerlies, was replete with an indoor barbecue built from rocks carried up from the beach – shale they were, reckoned to shatter and sure to splinter the family asunder, said the neighbours. Never happened, and the barbecue served as the centrepiece for many people for many years, serving blue groper, crays, and other catches from the sea, shamefully unprotected from our skindivers at the time.

A storm lifted the roof off the house shortly after construction, resulting in repairs that never quite sufficed. Holidays at Rosehill often became a comedy of buckets moved around to catch the leaks from the roof. The floor was damp and frequently replaced, starting with raw concrete then cork tiles, followed by blue lino tiles, until a new roof was installed and Mexican terracotta tiles laid to fix the problem, the final fix achieved after we persuaded Dad to dispense with his water-logged wine cellar beneath the floor.

In the early days, showers were taken in the space assigned for it behind the kitchen cupboard. It was equipped with a canvas camp shower, which more often gave up all its contents in one hearty turn of the rose, leaving the occupant soaped up with nowhere to go, and Dad exasperated by another failure in the family, particularly his unfortunate daughter-in-law, there because she had to be. Mostly we washed in the sea and rinsed in the trough.

The trip down the Clyde Mountain from Canberra always left the family covered in red dust, a necessary inconvenience always forgotten in the excitement of arrival, the group sigh, 'aah, there she is' (a physical thing) as the family car made it over the last rise to the point. Then, it was all out and down to the beach to wash off the dirt, before unpacking. Pride too, that once again, we had survived the trip and arrived at our Rosedale.

Sleeping was always an adventure. Mum and Dad shared the three-foot bed in the big room. There were only two rooms, the kitchen, dining and lounge room combined, and the kids' room. As Mum and Dad's bed was next to the bar, often they were forced to retire late, after our guests had moved on to their caravan accommodation in the carport. The kids' room was off the outdoor living, with an outside door of its own, giving independent 24-hour access to the world, an intended feature shared with our accommodation in Canberra. A series of sleeping arrangements was tried in the kids' apartment: double bunk stretcher capable of wild shaking to collapse, hammocks inside and out, pre-cut and child-assembled wooden bunks which often suffered the same fate as the stretcher. Mozzie coils controlled the kids' room climate, not always effective against hornets, huntsmen spiders, mice and rats. A lot of jumping and banging went on in the kids' room throughout the night, particularly if there were nervous child guests, but never disturbing Mum and Dad. This was our territory and we were in control, sort of.

The inside of the house was built by us, all of us, using hammers, saws, chisels and paint brushes, wielded equally by the ten and twelve-year-olds as their parents. Mum was the tradie, quick, clever and accurate, assisted by my brother aged twelve, but aided (sometimes, if permitted) by Dad and me. The proof of our efforts (Dad's and mine) was in evidence throughout the house. The rooms were lined in pine with canite (composition sugar cane) ceilings, sympathetic to the asbestos cement exterior walls and roof. Mum's curtains and Dad's 'Aboriginal' artworks completed the décor.

Of course, building never stopped as family members came up with new ideas about how they wanted Rosehill to look and feel. A room was added to serve as Mum's bedroom. She added it and Dad took it over on completion. The carport became a dormitory bedroom and the caravan was sold, a garage was added to become the ping pong room. A second storey room was built, and my brother moved in with his family. The toilet moved indoors next to a new, swish, bathroom when the Council ordered removal of the septic located on public land on the cliff front. An architect-designed ironbark pergola (not a sufficient title for the feature) adorned the new verandah, giving new charm to the view of the house from the road and adding to our pride of ownership, not necessarily always enhanced by the family washing strung on a line across it.

In recent times solar power was installed and awnings to reduce the glare for ageing occupants. New blinds replaced Mum's curtains and the bar was moved into the ping-pong room to make space for more sophisticated guests requiring a dining table. The kitchen was replaced and a laundry installed but the trough remained, preserving a tradition of bathing all small children at the trough, in front of the kitchen sink with a background view to the sea.

*

Now she's gone in the bushfire on New Year's Eve, 2019, and we weren't there to see her off. Our block on the cliff remains and we can still wash in the sea, maybe there can be a new camp shower. We had just painted her inside and out, so she looked her best. They say she exploded along with the houses either side. So, we start again ....

Helen Gamble, January 2020

'One lonely house intact
Among half a dozen razed to the ground,
Unrecognizable, blackened remnants of trees,
Jagged needles rising from ash-grey earth ...'

From 'The drive home' by Julia Kaylock
Published in *The Blue Nib*, 15 April 2020

'Shards of childhood curl in on themselves
Huddling in corrugated contortions
And nestling between clumps of rubble
Like frightened puppies ...'

From 'Rosedale, New Year's Eve' by Denise O'Hagan
Published in *Bluepepper*, 13 August 2020

About BlazeAid

BlazeAid is a volunteer-based national organisation that works with families and individuals in rural Australia following natural disasters such as fires and floods. As a result of the 2009 Black Saturday fires, Kevin and Rhonda Butler's East Kilmore farm was devastated. Needing to quickly secure their 1,500 sheep, they sought assistance from family, friends and local volunteers to help rebuild their fences. In the space of a week this was achieved, highlighting the strength of community.

Kevin and Rhonda's farm secured, they quickly set about working to rebuild fences and restore spirits locally, then spreading further and further afield. **BlazeAid was born.**

Since the devastation of the Black Saturday bushfires, thousands of long- and short-term BlazeAid volunteers have come from all parts of Australia, as well as New Zealand, Switzerland, England, Afghanistan, Canada, Germany, Austria, America and France to assist with the rebuilding of fences that have been damaged or destroyed.

In addition, Blazeaid provides a range of other relief services. Hot fires burn more than just fencing. It often sets back pasture production for years and farmers' ability to financially recover. Blazeaid also provides seed to approved applicants to help farms to become productive. In late 2020, they are commencing a huge project planting trees in paddocks. Kevin and Rhonda and their team are constantly attentive, meeting new challenges with each new year. BlazeAid volunteers can work in a disaster-affected area for many months, not only helping individuals and families, but also helping rebuild the local communities, helping to lift the spirits of people who are often facing their second or third flood event after years of drought, or devastating losses through bushfires.

'Not just rebuilding fences, but helping rebuild lives':

We asked you to come help us rebuild our fences but you guys have done way more than that, you have helped us rebuild our broken community. For that we are forever grateful to you and all the amazing volunteers. Maree Perkins, Monto, Qld

It was a true privilege to help the people of Cobargo, I travelled from the UK for 3 weeks and set up camp with Dean and Andy on the sports ground, not forgetting Peter too, so proud to been a part of it all and a honour to have met all you lovely Australians x. Lee Pallett, UK

Recognition of Services to Australia

On 14 August 2020, Her Majesty Queen Elizabeth awarded BlazeAid volunteers with the prestigious 'Commonwealth Point of Light' beacon award for outstanding volunteerism after the Australian 2020 Megafire. The award, personally signed by Her Majesty Queen Elizabeth, will be presented in Canberra by the British High Commissioner to Australia when it is safe to travel again.

I am delighted to virtually present Kevin and Rhonda Butler with this award for their dedication and commitment to both their own community and other communities in Australia who have been impacted by natural disasters – including the recent devastating bushfires. They both demonstrate incredible commitment to 'BlazeAid'; the volunteers they have recruited and the communities they support. They are making a significant impact on the lives of those that benefit from 'BlazeAid's work. All of you in the very impressive BlazeAid family should take a bow and feel very proud of the massive difference you make in the lives of others to help them after natural disasters. Your recognition is so well deserved and not before its time.

Vicki Treadell, British High Commissioner to Australia

BlazeAid is a registered Charity with PBI Status. A Public Benevolent Institution (PBI) is a type of charity which has a predominant (main) purpose of relieving needs arising from conditions such as poverty, sickness, distress or helplessness. This is known as providing 'benevolent relief'.

We have selected Blazeaid as the charity to which we will be donating the profits of this book, to assist them to undertake their great work supporting rural communities. As they will not be able to rely on volunteers from overseas over the coming fire danger period, they will be very happy for all the help they can get from Australians, whether it be in the form of dollars or person power.

Helping Communities Rebuild After Natural Disasters Since 2009
FIRE - FLOOD - DROUGHT – CYCLONE
www.blazeaid.com

Afterword

When we started out on this journey in January 2020 to create an anthology of bushfire poems we looked forward, as did the whole of Australia, to a time of renewal and rebuilding – a return to 'normal'. We rallied as a nation and, with assistance from around the world, we were confident we could overturn the disaster that had befallen us. Concerts were organised to raise funds; donations flooded in; people from distant shores provided person-power to assist in disaster recovery programs. A feeling of hope was in the air.

Little did we know that there would be scant time available for regrouping, or that 2020 would be a year in which further tides of 'unprecedented' events would challenge even the most rugged and resilient of Australians. We would not have imagined that recovery programs to rebuild lives, homes, businesses and farms would be further hampered by storms, floods and, soon enough, the arrival of COVID-19.

Of course, the pandemic has made its mark throughout the world, not just on Australia. Over the northern hemisphere summer, fires have burned while the virus raged. People have found themselves confined and isolated, dislocated and unable to return home, while those who had remained 'in place' were unable to visit friends and relatives, and many more lost jobs and livelihoods. Mental health has become an even more pressing issue as we face an uncertain future. Only time will tell us what changes need to be made to enable us to more effectively cohabit and to ensure continuance and greater nurturing of our rich biodiversity.

As we grapple with these bigger issues, we face another fire season, one that many experts predict will be as severe as the last, if not more so. This anthology is a 'snapshot in time', but we see it as part of a much bigger narrative: it is a story about the importance of community, of the growing realisation of the need to live sustainably and protect our fauna and flora. It is the story of Australia.

The Editors

www.ingramcontent.com/pod-product-compliance
Lightning Source LLC
Chambersburg PA
CBHW020319010526
44107CB00054B/1900